Progressive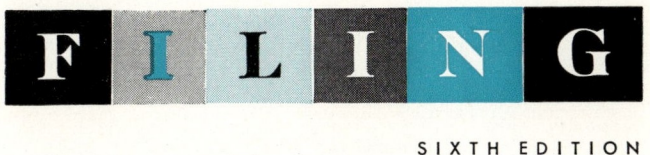

SIXTH EDITION

GILBERT KAHN, Ed.D.
Chairman, Business Department
East Side Commercial High School
Newark, New Jersey

THEODORE YERIAN, Ph.D.
Head, Department of Secretarial Studies
Oregon State College
Corvallis, Oregon

GREGG PUBLISHING DIVISION
McGraw-Hill Book Company, Inc.

New York   Chicago   San Francisco   Dallas   Toronto   London

PROGRESSIVE FILING, *Sixth Edition*

Copyright, © 1955, by McGraw-Hill Book Company, Inc. All rights reserved. This book, or parts thereof, may not be reproduced in any form without permission of the publishers. Copyright 1950, 1939, 1925, by Management Controls Division, Remington Rand Inc. July 1957-KP

Library of Congress Catalog No. 55-8903

PUBLISHED BY GREGG PUBLISHING DIVISION
McGraw-Hill Book Company, Inc.

Printed in the United States of America

Preface

The Need Filing is one of the most sought-after skills in today's business office. With the growth of business in the United States, the need for records has been greatly expanded. Probably no other activity in the business and government office has mushroomed so quickly as that of filing and records management. In fact, all clerical, stenographic, and secretarial positions—as well as specialized filing jobs—need business workers adequately trained in filing and finding records.

The Purpose *Progressive Filing*, Sixth Edition, is the successor to *Progressive Indexing and Filing*, Fifth Edition, published by Management Controls Division, Remington Rand Inc. As such, it retains the authenticity of its predecessor, a classic in the field.

Filing is a dynamic subject. Research into filing methods, filing procedures, and filing equipment is continuous. Methods of teaching filing are dynamic, too, and must be adapted to ever-changing curricula, schedules, and student needs and abilities. The primary purpose of *Progressive Filing*, Sixth Edition, is to provide authentic, up-to-date filing information that is easy to teach and easy to learn. It is designed with the teacher—and the student—in mind. It is geared to the classroom. Yet, in this revision, the authors have provided a treatment of filing methods, procedures, and equipment that will serve effectively as a reading and reference source for secretaries, office managers, and filing supervisors.

New Features *Progressive Filing*, Sixth Edition, contains new and outstanding features. Among these are:
- *Effective Condensation and Simplification of Rules.* The backbone of any filing instructional program is the presentation of the alphabetic filing rules. In this new edition, the authors have simplified the rules and have condensed the original thirty-three rules into twenty rules. The

rules are not changed in principle but are rearranged in order of presentation and are combined in some instances to take advantage of comparison and contrast in teaching and learning. Clear-cut examples are provided for each rule.

● *Teachable Presentation of Rules.* The rules are presented in Chapter 2, immediately after the learner is introduced to the general purpose and place of filing. The rules and their examples are presented in small "doses"—four in each section—followed immediately by two practice exercises. The first exercise for each section provides drill only on the new work presented in the section. The second exercise provides cumulative review on all the rules covered up to that point. This manner of presentation gives the student an opportunity to put into practice immediately the principles he has learned, thus cementing his knowledge of each rule. To give the student as much assistance as possible in the application of the rules, the appropriate rule number is given above the name to be alphabetized. This help continues through Rule 19.

The filing rules are reviewed cumulatively, beginning with Exercise 2. For example, in addition to the exercise for Rules 5, 6, 7, and 8, there is an additional exercise that reviews all rules presented up to that point. Thus, the student does not learn a rule and drop it. Each rule is recalled to him systematically through the exercises in Chapter 2.

● *Early Presentation of the Filing Cycle.* The text is organized so that the complete filing cycle is presented as early as possible in the course. Thus, if the school offers a very brief course in filing, every student still has an opportunity to work with all the basic aspects of filing procedure, such as all rules, cross references, charge-outs, and other filing procedures.

The text treats all the basic principles of filing that the general office worker should know. It is not the purpose of the typical filing course to train all students to become filing specialists. There is generally not the time, the interest, nor the *need* at this level of training for complete mastery of filing. After the basic elements have been learned, experience on the job becomes the best teacher.

● *Emphasis on Finding.* The real proof of correct filing is in the finding. One of the unique features of *Progressive Filing*, Sixth Edition, is the emphasis on finding as well as filing. Beginning with Exercise 11, and thereafter in all rule exercises, the student tests his filing by finding a group of names he has just filed.

● *Filing in the Small Office.* Emphasis in other instructional materials has been almost wholly devoted to filing in the large office. *Progressive*

Filing, Sixth Edition, takes cognizance of the fact that there are many problems and procedures that are peculiar to the small office; and the book devotes considerable attention to these problems and procedures. Information relative to filing in the small office is interwoven throughout the discussion in the text. Of particular importance, however, is the final chapter, "Establishing and Maintaining Filing Systems," which will be especially valuable to the worker in the small office.

● *Attractive Visual Aids.* The textbook is liberally illustrated with photographs, drawings, and other visual aids. The book was written and designed to make filing interesting and meaningful to the learner. Wherever an illustration could do a better job of describing a procedure or practice, it has been used in place of descriptive narrative. Many of the photographs and drawings were prepared especially for this book when standard illustrations did not meet the book's visual requirements.

● *Functional Use of Color.* The use of color, particularly in the treatment of the rules, serves a functional purpose as well as making the material more interesting.

Flexible Supporting Materials Special practice materials have been prepared to give the student realistic exercises in the application of filing rules, methods, and procedures. These are:

● *Workbook Exercises in Alphabetic Filing.* This 48-page workbook gives the student drills on alphabetic filing. Each of the twenty rules is presented and illustrated (just as in the textbook), followed by "cards" that are to be removed and filed in the proper order. In addition to the drills on rules, there are five review exercises embodying all the rules of alphabetic filing. In all, there are 720 names on "cards" for practice purposes.

● *Practice Materials in Progressive Filing—Basic Set.* This practice set contains cards and card guides for alphabetic card filing; folders and guides (in authentic color tabs) for Variadex Correspondence filing; guides and folders for numeric filing; collapsible boxes for card filing and correspondence filing; and cross-reference sheets and blank cards. This set is reusable.

● *Practice Materials in Progressive Filing—Advanced Set.* This practice set contains guides and folders for alphabetic subject filing; guides and folders for geographic filing; exercises in Triple-Check Automatic, decimal subject, and Soundex filing; and a collapsible correspondence filing box. Like the *Basic Set*, this set is also reusable.

- *Miniature Letters.* These seventy-five miniature letters are identical to the set prepared for the Remington Rand material. Carefully selected for their application of filing procedures, these letters include both incoming letters and "carbons" of outgoing letters. They furnish the student with examples of a wide range of activities involving the various steps in the filing program.
- *Practice Instruction Manual.* This booklet contains the instructions, examples, and procedures for working with the Practice Materials. It is published and distributed separately from the Practice Materials, since it may be used indefinitely.
- *Teacher's Manual and Key.* This manual is available to teachers of *Progressive Filing*, Sixth Edition. It contains teaching suggestions, schedules, and keys to the Practice Materials and the Workbook.

Acknowledgments   The authors wish to express their appreciation to many persons who have given assistance in preparing this filing program. Several members of the staff of Remington Rand Inc. co-operated wholeheartedly by reading the manuscript for the text and by giving expert guidance on the preparation of the practice materials.

All illustrations in the text were supplied by Remington Rand Inc. with a few exceptions. Credit is given to those exceptions below the illustration.

The authors have been privileged to base this new filing program on the materials published by the American Institute of Records Administration and hope that this joint effort will meet the exacting needs of teachers and students everywhere.

Gilbert Kahn
Theodore Yerian

Note: The name Remington Rand Inc. has been retained throughout this book when referring to that company's filing equipment and procedures, because the name is so well established among businessmen and educators. The complete name now is Remington Rand, Division of Sperry Rand Corporation.

Contents

	Preface	iii
1.	*Filing, the Memory of Business*	1
2.	*Indexing and Filing Rules*	8
3.	*Filing Procedures and Materials*	30
4.	*Alphabetic Correspondence Filing*	41
5.	*Charge Methods*	62
6.	*Transfer Methods*	69
7.	*Selection of Equipment and Supplies*	80
8.	*Numeric Correspondence Filing*	91
9.	*Geographic Correspondence Filing*	98
10.	*Subject Correspondence Filing*	104
11.	*Card and Visible Records*	113
12.	*Establishing and Maintaining Filing Systems*	124
	Summary of Basic Rules	144
	Index	147

In modern offices, files built for special needs make finding of material easy and fast.

Chapter 1

Filing—the "Memory" of Business

Who Needs Files?

▶ The businessman needs files and depends on them for important information—and he often needs that information in a hurry.

The general manager of the Apex Aircraft Company says to his secretary, "Miss Smith, get me the estimate from Wilson Brothers on that motion picture we're considering for our sales training classes. I need it for a board meeting this morning."

▶ The factory needs files for production control—accurate files that are used dozens of times every working day.

The factory supervisor asks his stock clerk, "John, how many carburetors were shipped to Denver last week? How many are on hand now? Chicago is on the phone, and they need this information."

1

▶ The doctor needs files constantly in consulting with his patients and with specialists.

Doctor Jameston says to his secretary-nurse, "Miss Warren, please get me the case-history file on Mr. Jenkins. He is coming in for a consultation at two."

▶ Every organization needs files—business, factory, government, charity—and every professional man—doctor, dentist, lawyer, architect—all depend on accurate filing records in their work. Today's office is a constant flow of papers—the written record is the "memory" of business.

This flow of papers comes from two sources: (1) From outside the organization—such as incoming correspondence, purchase invoices, statements; and (2) from inside the organization itself—such as carbon copies of outgoing letters, sales invoices, purchase orders, stock reports, and miscellaneous documents.

What Is Filing?

In a typical day, a business executive may need dozens of letters, reports, documents, and so on, as a basis for making intelligent decisions. In order to have these records available for quick reference, a system is needed in maintaining them. This system is filing.

If we were to define filing more fully, we would say that it is the process of classifying and arranging records so that they will be kept safely and will be obtainable quickly when needed. Filing is not merely the storing of records to get them out of sight, but a systematic organization of those records so that they can be located quickly.

A good filing system can often mean the difference between profit or loss for a businessman. If, for example, he cannot locate a source of information when he needs it, he may miss out on an opportunity for an important sale.

One of the purposes of filing is to preserve valuable records. You can imagine, for example, how important it is for insurance companies to maintain a safe place for records pertaining to their policyholders.

FILING—THE "MEMORY" OF BUSINESS

A card file used in an insurance company

The importance of preserving records is brought forcefully to our attention when we consider that 43 businesses out of 100 whose records were destroyed (by a fire or otherwise) were not able to resume business operations!

What Kinds of Records Are Kept?

Most of us think of letters—those received and carbon copies of those sent out—as the principal kind of record that is filed. While this is true in many offices, there are hundreds of different records for which files must be maintained. If you go to work in an architect's office, perhaps your most important file will be for blueprints. If you are secretary to a dentist, most of your records are kept on cards and filed in a card file. If you work for a commercial artist, your files may consist of drawings and art work—kept in oversize filing cabinets.

4 | PROGRESSIVE FILING

Every type of organization has files that are different from those in other organizations and fit its individual needs.

In a typical business, records are kept pertaining to accounting, personnel, sales, purchases, advertising, manufacturing, and general managerial activities. Each of these activities may have many different kinds of files and filing equipment for its special needs.

Filing, Then, Is Important

Filing has to do with one of the most important assets in an organization—its records. It is vital to every business worker.

For the Secretary. The secretary nearly always keeps files for her employer. And she is the person who is asked to locate material when her

An alphabetic file

FILING—THE "MEMORY" OF BUSINESS | 5

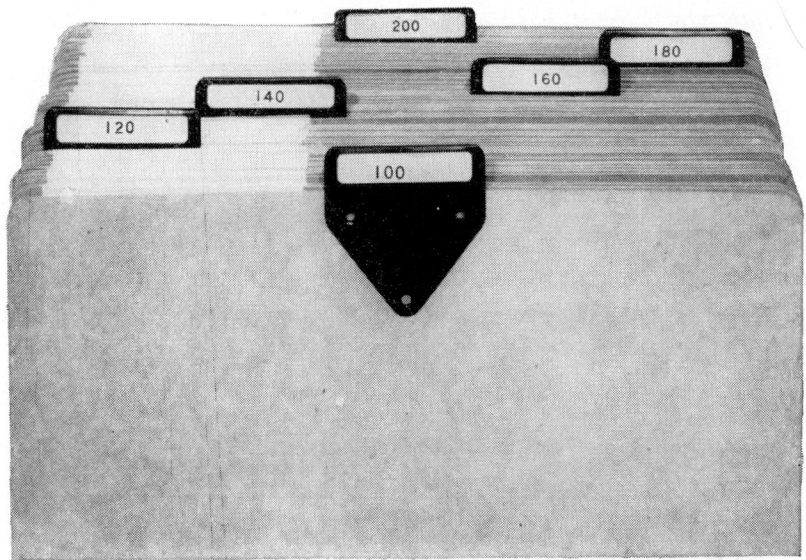

A numeric file

boss needs it. It goes without saying that the boss nearly always wants the records in a hurry—and her filing system must work! Often the secretary has the job of setting up a filing system where none existed before. If you were to go to work as secretary for a young lawyer who had just "hung out his shingle," you would need a good knowledge of filing rules and procedures!

For the General Office Worker. No matter whether you're employed as a bookkeeper, typist, salesman, or stenographer, you will use records in your work. These records must be filed in such a way that they can be located—either by yourself or a filing specialist. In a great many offices, general office workers are responsible for filing and finding their own materials.

For the File Clerk. In many organizations—particularly larger ones—files may be kept in one central location. These filing departments employ many workers whose sole job is to classify and file materials and to remove from the files material that is requested by other departments. In other words, some people make a career of filing. The opportunities for these positions are many, and they require special knowledge and skill.

What Methods of Filing Are Used?

There are actually only two bases for filing. One is *alphabetic*—which means filing material about persons or organizations according to the sequence of the alphabet. The other is *numeric*—filing by numbers.

All filing makes use of the alphabet; thus, geographic filing is filing alphabetically by city or territory, etc.; subject filing is filing alphabetically by the topic of the material rather than by the name of the person who originated it. Even numeric filing requires the aid of an al-

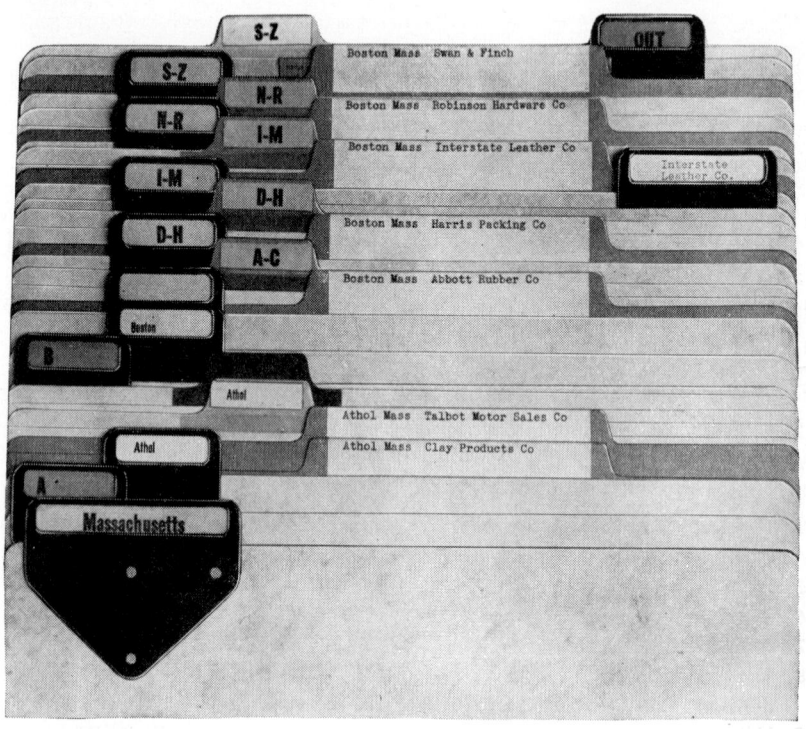

A geographic file

A subject file

phabetic index. These methods will be discussed in this book, and you will have an opportunity to see how each method serves a particular purpose.

QUESTIONS

for Review and Discussion

1. Why does business need files?
2. What are two sources of records?
3. What is the purpose of filing?
4. Mention three types of records that are filed.
5. Give examples of important records that must be preserved.
6. What are the bases for filing?
7. Mention two variations of these bases.
8. Why will the files kept by an architect be different from those kept by a dentist?
9. Why do you think it would be difficult for an organization to resume business operations when its files are destroyed?

Chapter 2

Indexing and Filing Rules

The Need for Standardization

If an office worker had his own individual method of filing material, he might be able to locate it rapidly when needed; but it is doubtful whether anyone else could. Typewriters with standard keyboards, regardless of the machine make, enable typists to use these machines. Basic filing rules have been developed so that anyone can put material into, or remove it rapidly from, the files in a typical office.

To meet the needs of special businesses or situations, it is sometimes necessary to vary a few of the basic rules, but any variations should be kept down to a minimum. Furthermore, any variations, once adopted, must be followed consistently by everyone using the particular files.

Alphabetic Arrangement

Alphabetic, geographic, subject, or combinations of these—have as their basis the alphabetic arrangement of names. Even numeric filing usually has names, subjects, or objects that must have some form of alphabetic index in addition to the numeric arrangement. The alphabetic arrangement of names means placing them in the same sequence as the letters of the alphabet. The three names *Baker*, *Jones*, and *Weber*, when listed in that order, are in alphabetic order because the first letter of *Baker* comes before the first letter of *Jones* in the alphabet, and the first letter of *Jones* comes before the first letter of *Weber* in the alphabet. *Butler* follows *Baker* in correct alphabetic order, because the second letter in *Baker* comes before the second letter in *Butler* in the alphabet, although the first letter in each name is the same.

Which Names Are Used in Alphabetic Arrangement?

Arranging names in alphabetic order is a simple matter when you know which names are to be compared. The location of the name *John Brown* in an alphabetic list of names would depend on which part of the name was considered first. The location of the name *Joseph LaZaro* in an alphabetic list of names would depend on whether *La* was considered as a separate name or as part of the last name *LaZaro*. It is the purpose of the basic rules of filing to help you make decisions of this type, so that you know which names are to be compared for alphabetic arrangement.

Two terms are used in these rules—unit and indexing.

A *unit* is any part of a name that is compared separately with parts of other names to determine filing arrangement. In the name *John Brown Company*, there are three units—*John*, *Brown*, and *Company*. In the name *Joseph LaZaro*, there are only two units—*Joseph* and *LaZaro*—because the *La* is not considered separately.

Indexing is determining the order in which to consider the units of a name. In *John Brown Company*, which of the three units should be compared first, second, and third with the units of other names? In *Joseph LaZaro*, which of the two units is to be considered first and which second? Because it is the purpose of the basic rules of filing to help determine filing units and the order in which those units should be considered, they are often referred to as "indexing and filing" rules.

The Basic Indexing and Filing Rules

There are twenty basic indexing and filing rules. To make it easier for you to learn them, they are presented on the following pages in five sections, with four rules in each section. At the end of each section, there are two exercises. The first exercise in each section provides practice in applying the rules taught in that section. The second exercise in each section drills on all the rules learned up to that point. To give you assistance, if you need it, the number of the indexing and filing rule involved has been placed above each name to be filed.

SECTION ONE

RULE 1

NAMES OF INDIVIDUALS. Transpose the names of individuals. Consider the surname (last name) first, the given name (first name) second, and the middle name, if any, third.

NAME	CORRECT FILING ARRANGEMENT
Nora Carolyn Phillips	Phillips, Nora Carolyn
John Thompson	Thompson, John

RULE 2

ALPHABETIC ORDER. Each word in a name is an indexing unit. Arrange the names in alphabetic order by comparing similar units in each name. Consider the second units only when the first units are identical. Consider the third units only when both the first and second units are identical.

NAME	CORRECT FILING ARRANGEMENT		
	UNIT 1	UNIT 2	UNIT 3
Richard Adams	Adams	Richard	
Alice Ruth Buckley	Buckley	Alice	Ruth
John Carl Buckley	Buckley	John	Carl
John Peter Buckley	Buckley	John	Peter

RULE 3

SINGLE SURNAMES OR INITIALS. A surname, when used alone, precedes the same surname with a first name or initial. A surname with a first initial only precedes a surname with a complete first name. This rule is sometimes stated, "Nothing comes before something."

CORRECT FILING ARRANGEMENT

NAME	UNIT 1	UNIT 2
Adams	Adams	
Richard Adams	Adams	Richard
A. Buckley	Buckley	A.
Alice Buckley	Buckley	Alice

RULE 4

SURNAME PREFIXES. A surname prefix is *not* a separate indexing unit, but it is considered part of the surname. These prefixes include: *d', D', Da, de, De, Del, Des, Di, Du, Fitz, La, Le, M', Mac, Mc, O', St., Van, Van der, Von, Von der,* and others. The prefixes *M', Mac,* and *Mc* are indexed and filed exactly as they are spelled. The prefix *St.* is indexed and filed as though spelled out.

CORRECT FILING ARRANGEMENT

NAME	UNIT 1	UNIT 2	UNIT 3
Phillip J. Deems	Deems	Phillip	J.
Vincent DeLuca	DeLuca	Vincent	
Dorothy Mack	Mack	Dorothy	
William L. MacPherson	MacPherson	William	L.
William L. McPherson	McPherson	William	L.

Filing Practice

If you have been supplied with the practice set, *Practice Materials for Progressive Filing, Basic Set,* you should now consult your *Instruction Manual* for directions on how to complete Exercise 1 and all other practice exercises for the basic indexing and filing rules. If you have

12 | PROGRESSIVE FILING

not been supplied with the practice set, follow the instructions given below.

1. Write each of the following names in correct indexing form on a separate 5 by 3 card. The identification number of the name is to be placed in the upper right-hand corner.

    The typed name should start on the third space from the left edge of the card. If you are using ruled cards, it should be placed on the first printed rule. If you are using unruled cards, it should be started on the second line space from the top.

```
Brown, Martin
```

Name typed on unruled card

```
Brown, Martin
```

Name typed on ruled card

2. Arrange the ten cards in alphabetic sequence.
3. List the numbers of the cards in the order in which you arranged them on an answer sheet similar to the one illustrated on page 13. Hand in this answer sheet to your teacher for checking.
4. Save the ten index cards for use in Exercise 14.

INDEXING AND FILING RULES | 13

```
Name  Mary Jones                Exercise No.  1
         1.  5              6.
         2.  2              7.
         3.  6              8.
         4.  10             9.
         5.                10.
```

A partially completed answer sheet

EXERCISE 1 Remember, to give you assistance, if you need it, the number of the indexing and filing rule involved has been placed above each name.

1. Dorothy S. Damar [1, 2, 3]
2. Samuel Abbey [1, 2]
3. Martin Brown [1, 2]
4. Dorothy Damar [1, 2]
5. Philip Abbey [1, 2]
6. Brown [1, 2, 3]
7. Fred Da Mato [1, 2, 4]
8. Frederick D'Amato [1, 2, 4]
9. Thomas Browne [1, 2]
10. M. Brown [1, 2, 3]

EXERCISE 2 Index and file cards for names 11-20 and hand in an answer sheet. Save the cards for use in Exercise 14. Remember, to give you assistance, if you need it, the number of the indexing and filing rule involved has been placed above each name.

11. H. Bar [1, 2, 3]
12. Gregory Carroll [1, 2]
13. Grace Ayers [1, 2]
14. Harry Bar [1, 2]
15. George Ayres [1, 2]
16. Robert Du Pont [1, 2, 4]
17. Thomas Carrol [1, 2]
18. Ayers [1, 2, 3]
19. R. Dupont [1, 2, 3]
20. Thomas H. Carrol [1, 2, 3]

SECTION TWO

RULE 5 — NAMES OF FIRMS. Names of firms and institutions are indexed and filed exactly as they are written when they do not contain the *complete* name of an individual.

CORRECT FILING ARRANGEMENT

NAME	UNIT 1	UNIT 2	UNIT 3
Center Grocery Company	Center	Grocery	Company
Center Hardware Store	Center	Hardware	Store
Curtis Secretarial School	Curtis	Secretarial	School

RULE 6 — NAMES OF FIRMS CONTAINING COMPLETE INDIVIDUAL NAMES. When the firm or institution name includes the *complete* name of an individual, the units are transposed for indexing in the same way as the name of an individual.

CORRECT FILING ARRANGEMENT

NAME	UNIT 1	UNIT 2	UNIT 3	UNIT 4
Drew Fruit Store	Drew	Fruit	Store	
John Drew Lumber Company	Drew	John	Lumber	Company
Arthur Miller Corporation	Miller	Arthur	Corporation	
Miller Milk Company	Miller	Milk	Company	

RULE 7 — ARTICLE "THE." When *The* occurs at the beginning of a name, it is placed at the end in parentheses when writing names on cards and folders; if in the middle, it is placed in parentheses but is not moved. In both cases, it is *not* an indexing unit and is disregarded in filing.

INDEXING AND FILING RULES | 15

CORRECT FILING ARRANGEMENT

NAME	UNIT 1	UNIT 2	UNIT 3
Andrew the Baker	Andrew (the)	Baker	
The Charles Baker Corporation	Baker	Charles	Corporation (The)
The Baker Dairy	Baker	Dairy (The)	

RULE 8

HYPHENATED NAMES. Hyphenated firm names are considered as *separate* indexing units. Hyphenated surnames of individuals are considered as *one* indexing unit; this applies also to hyphenated names of individuals whose complete names are part of a firm name.

CORRECT FILING ARRANGEMENT

NAME	UNIT 1	UNIT 2	UNIT 3
Lee-Barry Garage	Lee	Barry	Garage
John Lee-Barry	Lee-Barry	John	
The John Lee-Barry Company	Lee-Barry	John	Company

EXERCISE 3 Index and file cards for names 21-30 and hand in an answer sheet. Save the cards for use in Exercise 14. Remember, to give you assistance, if you need it, the number of the indexing and filing rule involved has been placed above each name.

21. Christie-Lewis Bakery [5, 8]
22. Ayers Rubber Company [5]
23. The Dunwoody Tile Company [5, 7]
24. The Charles Carroll-Blake Antique Shop [7, 8, 6]
25. The Alfred Ayers Company [6, 7]
26. The Christie Storage Company [5, 7]
27. Carroll-Blake Publishing Company [5, 8]
28. Anne Christie-Lewis [8]
29. Charles Carroll-Blake [8]
30. Fred Dunwoody Book Store [6]

EXERCISE 4 Index and file cards for names 31-40 and hand in your answer sheet. Save the cards for use in Exercise 14. Remember, to give you assistance, the number of the indexing and filing rule involved has been placed above each name.

31. The Christy Loan Company 5, 7
32. Dunworth-Leech Beauty Parlor 5, 8
33. The Christian Engineering Company 5, 7
34. Arthur Abbott 1, 2
35. The Abbott Screen Company 5, 7
36. Freda D'Amato 1, 2, 4
37. Walter Abbe 1, 2
38. The Milton Christie Realty Company 6, 7
39. Arlene Dunworth-Leech 1, 2, 8
40. Da Mato 3, 4

SECTION THREE

RULE 9
ABBREVIATIONS. Abbreviations are considered as though the name were written in full; however, single letters other than abbreviations are considered as separate indexing units.

CORRECT FILING ARRANGEMENT

NAME	UNIT 1	UNIT 2	UNIT 3	UNIT 4
ABC Products	A	B	C	Products
Chas. Atlas	Atlas	Charles		
CIT Corp.	C	I	T	Corporation
St. George Hotel	Saint	George	Hotel	
Robert Scott	Scott	Robert		

RULE 10
CONJUNCTIONS, PREPOSITIONS, AND FIRM ENDINGS. Conjunctions and prepositions, such as *and, for, in, of,* are disregarded in indexing and filing but are not omitted or their order changed when writing names on cards and folders.

Firm endings, such as *Ltd., Inc., Co., Son, Bros., Mfg.,* and *Corp.,* are treated as a unit in indexing and filing and are considered as though spelled in full, such as *Brothers* and *Incorporated.*

INDEXING AND FILING RULES | 17

CORRECT FILING ARRANGEMENT

NAME	UNIT 1	UNIT 2	UNIT 3
Harris Co., Ltd.	Harris	Company	Limited
Jones and Smith	Jones	Smith	
William Peters & Son	Peters	William	Son
Macleod & Co., Inc.	Macleod	Company	Incorporated

RULE 11

ONE OR TWO WORDS. Names that may be spelled as one word, as two words, or hyphenated are indexed and filed as *one word*.

CORRECT FILING ARRANGEMENT

NAME	UNIT 1	UNIT 2	UNIT 3
Inter State Bus Co.	Interstate	Bus	Company
Interstate Trucking Co.	Interstate	Trucking	Company
Northeast High School	Northeast	High	School
North East Weaving Mills	Northeast	Weaving	Mills

RULE 12

COMPOUND GEOGRAPHIC NAMES. Compound geographic names are considered as separate indexing and filing units, except when the first part of the name is not an English word, such as the *Los* in *Los Angeles*.

CORRECT FILING ARRANGEMENT

NAME	UNIT 1	UNIT 2	UNIT 3	UNIT 4
Des Moines Shoe Co.	Des Moines	Shoe	Company	
New Haven Clock Co.	New	Haven	Clock	Company
New Jersey News Co.	New	Jersey	News	Company

PROGRESSIVE FILING

EXERCISE 5 Index and file cards for names 41-50 and hand in your answer sheet. Save the cards for use in Exercise 14.

41. Air Port Florist [11]
42. Battle Creek Market [12]
43. Brown Mfg. Co. [9, 10]
44. Jos. Barber [9]
45. ABC Oil Co. [9, 10]
46. Abbott and Brown [10]
47. Bar Harbor Fisheries [12]
48. Airport Restaurant [11]
49. Brown of Hollywood [10]
50. Brown Meat Corp. [9, 10]

EXERCISE 6 Index and file cards for names 51-60 and hand in your answer sheet. Save the cards for use in Exercise 16.

51. Broad Cloth Weavers [5, 11]
52. M. H. Fitzgerald [1, 3, 4]
53. Broadcloth Spinning Mills [5, 11]
54. Cedar Rapids Tile Company [5, 10, 12]
55. Flanagan-Holland Supply House [5, 8]
56. Calif. Fruit Co. [5, 9, 10]
57. Cedarhurst Taxi [5]
58. Flanagan and Sons [5, 10]
59. Murray Fitz Gerald [1, 4]
60. The Fred Flanagan-Holland Loan Co. [6, 7, 8, 10]

SECTION FOUR

RULE 13 TITLES OR DEGREES. Titles or degrees of individuals, whether preceding or following the name, are *not* considered in indexing or filing. They are placed in parentheses after the given name or initial. Terms that designate seniority, such as *Jr., Senior, 2d*, are also placed in parentheses and are considered for indexing and filing only when the names to be indexed are otherwise identical.

Exception A: When the name of an individual consists of a title and one name only, such as *Queen Elizabeth*, it is *not* transposed and the title *is* considered for indexing and filing.

Exception B: When a title or foreign article is the initial word of a firm or association name, it *is* considered for indexing and filing.

INDEXING AND FILING RULES | 19

CORRECT FILING ARRANGEMENT

NAME	UNIT 1	UNIT 2	UNIT 3	UNIT 4
Il Commercio Publishing Co.	Il	Commercio	Publishing	Company
Prince George	Prince	George		
Prince George Fisheries	Prince	George	Fisheries	
Dr. Henry Prince	Prince	Henry		
John Prince, Jr.	Prince	John	Junior	
John Prince, Sr.	Prince	John	Senior	

RULE 14

POSSESSIVES. When a word ends in *apostrophe s*, the *s* is *not* considered in indexing and filing. However, when a word ends in *s apostrophe*, because the *s* is part of the original word, it *is* considered. This rule is sometimes stated, "Consider everything up to the apostrophe."

CORRECT FILING ARRANGEMENT

NAME	UNIT 1	UNIT 2	UNIT 3
Myer's Oxygen Service	Myer	Oxygen	Service
Thomas B. Myer	Myer	Thomas	B.
Myers' Paint Store	Myers'	Paint	Store
Henry Myerson	Myerson	Henry	

RULE 15

U. S. AND FOREIGN GOVERNMENT NAMES. Names pertaining to the Federal Government are indexed and filed under *United States Government* and then subdivided by title of the department, bureau, division, commission, or board.

Names pertaining to foreign governments are indexed and filed under names of countries and then subdivided by title of the department, bureau, division, commission, or board.

Phrases, such as *Department of, Bureau of, Division of, Commission of, Board of,* when used in titles of governmental bodies, are placed in parentheses after the word they modify but are *disregarded* in indexing and filing. Such phrases, however, *are* considered in indexing and filing nongovernmental names.

CORRECT FILING ARRANGEMENT

NAME	UNIT 1	UNIT 2	UNIT 3	UNIT 4	UNIT 5
Committee for World Travel	Committee	World	Travel		
Kingdom of Sweden Ministry of Defense	Sweden	Defense			
U. S. Dept. of Agriculture	United	States	Government	Agriculture	
U. S. Dept. of Commerce, Bureau of Census	United	States	Government	Commerce	Census
Republic of Uruguay, Dept. of Trade	Uruguay	Trade			

RULE 16 OTHER POLITICAL SUBDIVISIONS.

Names pertaining to other political subdivisions, such as states, counties, cities, or towns, are indexed and filed under the name of the political subdivision and then subdivided by the title of the department, bureau, division, commission, or board.

CORRECT FILING ARRANGEMENT

NAME	UNIT 1	UNIT 2	UNIT 3	UNIT 4
Board of Education, New York City	New	York	City	Education
Dept. of Education, New York State	New	York	State	Education
Bureau of Weights and Measures, State of Oregon	Oregon	State	Weights	Measure
Water Dept., Town of Verona, New Jersey	Verona	Town	Water	

EXERCISE 7 Index and file cards for names 61-70 and hand in your answer sheet. Save the cards for use in Exercise 16.

61. U. S. Dept. of Commerce [15]
62. Brother Lucius [13]
63. Bureau of Economic Education, Inc. [15]
64. Egan's Mirror Co. [14]
65. El Commercio Publishing Co. [13]
66. Egans' Pharmacy [14]
67. Walter Egan, Jr. [13]
68. Kingdom of Ethiopia, Ministry of State [15]
69. City of Buffalo, Dept. of Public Works [16]
70. Doctor Walter Egan [13]

EXERCISE 8 Index and file cards for names 71-90 and hand in your answer sheet. Save the cards for use in Exercise 16.

71. Flanagan's Moving Co. [5, 9, 10, 14]
72. Eastside Tobacco Co. [5, 9, 10, 11]
73. Republic of France, Dept. of Finance [15]
74. Friendly Service and Repairs [5, 10]
75. Conrad-Moran Lumber Co. [5, 8, 9, 10]
76. Professor Fitzgerald [3, 4, 13]
77. Friendly Service, Inc. [5, 9, 10]
78. Flowers for the Home, Inc. [5, 9, 10]
79. Flanagans' Hardware Co. [5, 14]
80. Charles The Barber [5, 7]
81. Chas. Flowers [1, 9]
82. Father Fitzgerald [4, 13]
83. M. Fitz Gerald [1, 3, 4]
84. East Side Trucking Co. [5, 9, 10, 11]
85. U. S. Dept. of Agriculture, Bureau of Animal Industry [12, 15]
86. City of El Paso, Dept. of Public Safety [12, 16]
87. F and G Furniture Store [3, 5, 10]
88. Countess Elaine Face Powder Co. [5, 13]
89. M. Howard Fitzgerald [1, 3, 4]
90. Lewis Conrad-Moran Restaurant [6, 8]

SECTION FIVE

RULE 17 NUMBERS. Any number in a name is considered as though it were written in words, and it is indexed and filed as *one* unit.

CORRECT FILING ARRANGEMENT

NAME	UNIT 1	UNIT 2	UNIT 3
71st Street Garage	Seventy-first	Street	Garage
The 6th Street Building	Sixth	Street	Building
The 6th Street Theater	Sixth	Street	Theater
Warehouse on 22nd Street	Warehouse	Twenty-second	Street

RULE 18 ADDRESSES. When the same name appears with different addresses, the names are indexed as usual and arranged alphabetically according to city or town. The state is considered only when there is duplication of both individual or company name and city name. If the same name is located at different addresses within the same city, then the names are arranged alphabetically by streets. If the same name is located at more than one address on the same street, then the names are arranged from the lower to the higher street number.

CORRECT FILING ARRANGEMENT

NAME	UNIT 1	UNIT 2	UNIT 3	UNIT 4	UNIT 5
Grant Stores 20 East St., Boston	Grant	Stores	Boston	East, 20	Street
Grant Stores 936 East St., Boston	Grant	Stores	Boston	East, 936	Street
Grant Stores West Ave., Boston	Grant	Stores	Boston	West	Avenue
Grant Stores, Newark, Del.	Grant	Stores	Newark	Delaware	
Grant Stores, Newark, Ohio	Grant	Stores	Newark	Ohio	
Grant Stores, Philadelphia	Grant	Stores	Philadelphia		

INDEXING AND FILING RULES | 23

RULE 19

BANK NAMES. Because the names of many banking institutions are alike in several respects, as *First National Bank, Second National Bank*, etc., banks are indexed and filed first by city location, then by bank name, with the state location written on a card or a folder in parentheses and considered only if necessary.

CORRECT FILING ARRANGEMENT

NAME	UNIT 1	UNIT 2	UNIT 3	UNIT 4
First National Bank, Miami, Florida	Miami	First	National	Bank
First National Bank, Mobile, Alabama	Mobile	First	National	Bank
Ironbound Trust Co., Newark, N. J.	Newark	Ironbound	Trust	Company

RULE 20

MARRIED WOMEN. The legal name of a married woman is the one used for filing purposes. Legally, a man's surname is the only part of a man's name a woman assumes when she marries. Her legal name, therefore, could be either: (1) her own first and middle names together with her husband's surname, or (2) her own first name and maiden surname together with her husband's surname. *Mrs.* is placed in parentheses after the name when writing on a card or folder. Her husband's first and middle names are given in parentheses below her legal name.

CORRECT FILING ARRANGEMENT

NAME	UNIT 1	UNIT 2	UNIT 3
Mrs. Robert C. Egan (Helen Ann)	Egan,	Helen	Ann
Mrs. Allen F. Walker (Rose Vivian)	Walker,	Rose	Vivian

EXERCISE 9 Index and file cards for names 91-100. Hand in an answer sheet. Save the cards for use in Exercise 16.

24 | PROGRESSIVE FILING

91. Cedare Brothers, River Avenue, Hartford, Conn.[18]
92. First National Bank, Broadside, Pa.[19]
93. 4th Street Hotel[17]
94. Mrs. John David Charles (Ellen Walters)[20]
95. Cedare Brothers, Main Street, Hartford, Conn.[18]
96. People's Trust Co., Boston, Mass.[19]
97. Cedare Brothers, Norwalk, Conn.[18]
98. Mrs. Henry A. Charles (Rose Smith)[20]
99. First National Bank, Broadside, Maine[19]
100. 5th Avenue Bakery[17]

Cross Reference

Different names or subjects may be used in calling for a piece of correspondence or some information in a card file. Since the folder containing the correspondence, or the card with the information, can be filed in only one place, it is necessary to have references under all other headings by which the file may be requested. These references may be either on cards or sheets, depending on the type of file used. On these cards or sheets a notation is made to *see* the heading under which the material is actually filed. This procedure is called *cross reference*. Suppose a firm name had been changed from Harold Miller Leather Goods Company to Ace Leather Goods, Incorporated. In a card file, as shown by the illustration, there would be the original card for the Harold Miller Leather Goods Company and also one for Ace Leather Goods, Incorporated. For an illustration of a cross-reference sheet, see page 35.

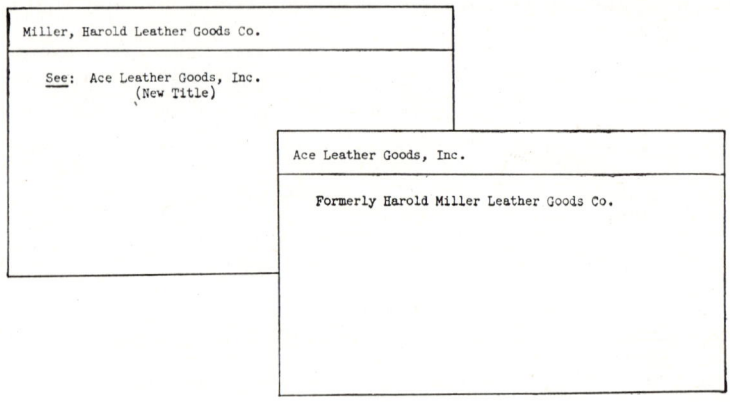

INDEXING AND FILING RULES | 25

EXERCISE 10

1. Index cards for names 101 through 150. As you do so, cross-reference the following names.
   (*a*) Captain Bill's Show Boat, card 106; cross-reference under William Boyle, card 106x.
   (*b*) Mrs. David B. Brent, card 116; cross-reference under Louise Bentley, card 116x.
   (*c*) Bar-Brass Manufacturers, card 132; cross-reference under Brass-Bar Manufacturers, card 132x.
   (*d*) Bureau of Awning Manufacturers of America, card 139; cross-reference under Awning Manufacturers' Bureau of America, card 139x.
2. Arrange the cards in correct alphabetic sequence. The cross-reference cards will, of course, be placed where the first unit of the name on the card occurs in the alphabet. In other words, card 106 will be filed with the "C's" while card 106x will be filed in the "B's."
3. Submit an answer sheet. The cross-reference cards will be listed in addition to the regular cards.

101. Brazil-Lawrence Corp.
102. Carl Bonde
103. Artcraft Hobby Co.
104. Addison-Jackson Paper Co., Mobile, Alabama
105. Mrs. James C. Brent (Alice Helen)
106. Captain Bill's Show Boat
107. Bond Roofing Company
108. State of Arkansas, Forestry Service
109. Art Craft Knitting and Sewing Shop
110. Republic of Brazil, Dept. of Justice
111. The American Metal Construction Co.
112. Amer. Radiator Co.
113. Rufus Bond
114. Wilson C. Allen
115. William Allen
116. Mrs. David B. Brent (Louise Bentley)
117. Board of Missionary Preparation
118. American Metal Box Co.
119. Agolia's 10 and 25¢ Store
120. The Blue Seal Company
121. Allen's Beauty Shop
122. C-M Hosiery Mills
123. Robert Bond
124. Blue Seal Washing Fluid Co.
125. Blue Seal Cleaning Stores
126. Billing and Collecting Service
127. David Benson
128. Billings' Bakery Shop

26 | PROGRESSIVE FILING

129. City of Buffalo, Dept. of Public Safety
130. Arkansas Vending Corp.
131. William C. Agolia
132. Bar-Brass Manufacturers
133. David C. Benson
134. Addisons' Butter Co.
135. Barbers' Supplies, Inc.
136. Bud's Men's Shop
137. Buffalo Meter Co.
138. Car Equipment Co.
139. Bureau of Awning Manufacturers of America
140. Arthur Benson
141. Dominion of Canada, Dept. of Interior
142. Car Equip. & Supply Co.
143. Budget Home Utilities Co.
144. Samuel Brook-Thompson
145. Samuel Brook-Thompson Thread Co.
146. Mrs. Walter D. Addison (Mary C.)
147. Canadian Fur Shop
148. Dominion of Canada, Dept. of Agriculture
149. Brook Springs Bread Co.
150. Addison-Jackson Paper Co., Harrisburg, Pa.

EXERCISE 11—Practice in Finding The real proof of correct filing is in the finding. Speed in finding is most essential in a business office, for some worker's time will be wasted if he has to wait until a record he needs can be located.

See how fast you can find the following cards filed in Exercise 10. On a sheet of paper, write the names and card numbers in four columns similar to the way it has been done in the following illustration. Hand in this answer sheet to your teacher for checking.

1. Captain Bill's Show Boat
2. David Benson
3. William C. Agolia
4. American Radiator Company

Card No.	Name	Filed After Card No.	Filed Before Card No.
166	David C. Benson	134	168

A partially completed answer sheet

5. C-M Hosiery Mills
6. The Blue Seal Co.
7. Louise Bentley
8. Dept. of Interior, Canada
9. Samuel Brook-Thompson Thread Co.
10. Artcraft Hobby Co.

EXERCISE 12

1. Index cards for names 151-200 and cross-reference:
   (*a*) Franklin the Druggist, card 157; cross-reference under William Franklin, card 157x.
   (*b*) Federation of Churches, card 164; cross-reference under Church Federation, card 164x.
   (*c*) Committee for the Conservation of Natural Resources, card 159; cross-reference under Conservation of Natural Resources Committee, card 159x.
   (*d*) Charles the Hairdresser, card 182; cross-reference under Charles Denton, card 182x.
2. Arrange the cards in correct alphabetic sequence.
3. Hand in an answer sheet.

151. The 50 Club
152. Kingdom of Denmark, Ministry of Trade
153. J. R. Decker
154. Citizens Trust Co., Flint, Mich.
155. Conroy Brick Co.
156. Essex Co., 75 Broad St., Jackson, Miss.
157. Franklin The Druggist
158. State of Connecticut, Commission for the Blind
159. Committee for the Conservation of Natural Resources
160. L. J. Dandrea
161. The 85th Anniversary Committee
162. Findley
163. Rev. L. Findlay
164. Federation of Churches
165. Commerce Investment Co.
166. Harold Easton-Bailey
167. The Crosstown Messenger Service
168. Leonard Du Mont
169. Duffy's Place
170. Essex Co., 402 Broad St., Jackson, Miss.
171. Conroy Bldg. & Loan Assn.
172. Clear Bay Boat Corp.
173. The Cuba-American Sugar Co.
174. El Producto Tobacco Products
175. State of Connecticut, Dept. of Education
176. Church of the Epiphany

28 | PROGRESSIVE FILING

177. Chemical Analysis Laboratories
178. City of Du Bois, Road Dept.
179. The Committee of 5
180. 18 Caledonia St. Bldg.
181. Commercial Consultants, Inc.
182. Charles The Hairdresser
183. Prof. Arnold Cleary
184. Church Travel Bureau
185. Chemical Co. of America
186. First National Bank, Franklin, N. J.
187. U. S. Government, Dept. of Agriculture, Bureau of Fruits and Vegetables
188. City of De Kalb, Dept. of Parks
189. The 4 Seas Co.
190. L. James D'Andrea
191. Dime Savings Bank, Easton, Pa.
192. Major Vincent Duffy
193. Ft. Wayne Hotel
194. Republic of Cuba, Dept. of Defense
195. Dubois and Sons
196. 5 Corners Garage
197. The Cross Town Bus Co.
198. First National Bank, Franklin, Maryland
199. 40 Brands, Inc.
200. Louis Findlay

EXERCISE 13 See how fast you can find the following cards among those you filed in Exercise 12. On a sheet of paper, write the names and card numbers in four columns similar to the way it has been done in the illustration on page 26. Hand in this answer sheet to your teacher for checking.

1. L. J. Dandrea
2. Commercial Consultants, Inc.
3. 18 Caledonia St. Bldg.
4. Ft. Wayne Hotel
5. Dime Savings Bank, Easton, Pa.
6. Franklin The Druggist
7. Dept. of Education, Conn.
8. Duffy's Place
9. Church Travel Bureau
10. The 50 Club

EXERCISE 14—For Additional Practice in Filing
1. Arrange in correct alphabetic sequence cards 1-50.
2. Hand in an answer sheet.

EXERCISE 15—For Additional Practice in Finding See how fast you can find the following cards among those you filed in Exercise

14. On a sheet of paper, write the names and card numbers in four columns similar to the way it has been done in the illustration on page 26. Hand in this answer sheet to your teacher for checking.

1. Brown Mfg. Co.
2. George Ayres
3. Christie-Lewis Bakery
4. Abbott and Brown
5. Freda D'Amato
6. Thomas H. Carrol
7. The Christy Loan Company
8. Charles Carroll-Blake
9. Airport Restaurant
10. H. Bar

EXERCISE 16—For Additional Practice in Filing
1. Arrange in correct alphabetic sequence cards 51-100.
2. Hand in an answer sheet.

EXERCISE 17—For Additional Practice in Finding See how fast you can find the following cards among those you filed in Exercise 16. On a sheet of paper, write the names and card numbers in four columns similar to the way it has been done in the illustration on page 26. Hand in this answer sheet to your teacher for checking.

1. Eastside Tobacco Co.
2. City of Buffalo, Public Works Dept.
3. 5th Avenue Bakery
4. Bureau of Economic Education
5. Murray Fitz Gerald
6. 1st National Bank, Broadside, Pa.
7. Cedare Brothers, Norwalk, Conn.
8. Flanagan's Moving Co.
9. Friendly Service, Inc.
10. Charles The Barber

QUESTIONS

for Review and Discussion

1. Why is standardization necessary in filing?
2. What is the basis of all methods of filing?
3. What is meant by the following terms:
   (a) unit? (b) indexing? (c) given name? (d) surname?
4. What is a surname prefix?
5. What is the legal name of a married woman?
6. What is "cross-referencing"?

Chapter 3

Filing Procedures and Materials

Vertical Correspondence Filing

The operation of a business, large or small, requires communication both within the business itself and with other organizations. This communication takes the form of letters, telegrams, orders, invoices, bills, checks, reports, and miscellaneous papers. For purposes of filing, all this material is considered as correspondence, even though in a true dictionary sense *correspondence* refers to letters only. This over-all definition of correspondence is used to distinguish the filing of such papers from card filing.

In modern business, correspondence is filed on edge, or vertically, just like cards. In older methods of filing, papers were piled flat, one on top of the other. This necessitated the handling of many papers before one paper could be found or removed. With vertical filing, each

Illustration courtesy Mutual Life Insurance Co.

paper can be handled independently, thus making possible greater speed, accuracy, and accessibility.

Card filing is the simplest form of vertical filing, because there is usually only one name on each card; and each card is separate and distinct from every other card. As you have already discovered from your work in Chapter 2, the filing and finding of cards simply involves the application of the basic indexing and filing rules to the one name on each card. Correspondence filing, however, calls for making more decisions. More than one name is used in the average piece of correspondence; it must, therefore, first be analyzed to determine under which of the names it is to be filed. Secondly, when that name has been selected, the basic indexing and filing rules must be applied. Finally, because there will be other related material filed under the same name, the paper must be filed in proper sequence within the category. It can be said, then, that the *vertical filing* of correspondence is the bringing together, in one place, of all correspondence to, from, or about one individual, one firm, one place, or one subject, and filing it on edge, usually in folders and behind guides; this makes for speed, accuracy, and accessibility.

Procedures Preliminary to Filing

It is exceedingly important that in every business some routine be established to provide for the regular and reliable collection of all papers to be filed. Experience reveals that many missing or hard-to-locate documents can be lost or misplaced prior to the actual filing operation. This collection routine should be the same whether the organization is large with separate mailing and filing departments, each with many employees, or whether the office is small and nondepartmentalized, with one or two workers. The difference lies only in the number of people involved: whereas in a small office one person might perform every step in the routine, in a larger organization the various steps become the responsibility of a number of workers.

All incoming correspondence, except personal mail, should be opened and time-stamped. Although this marking can be done by hand, most offices use a machine or rubber stamp. This stamp records the date, so that responsibility can be fixed for the lapse of time between the day

32 | PROGRESSIVE FILING

the letter was received and the day it was answered. The correspondence should then be delivered promptly to the proper person for attention.

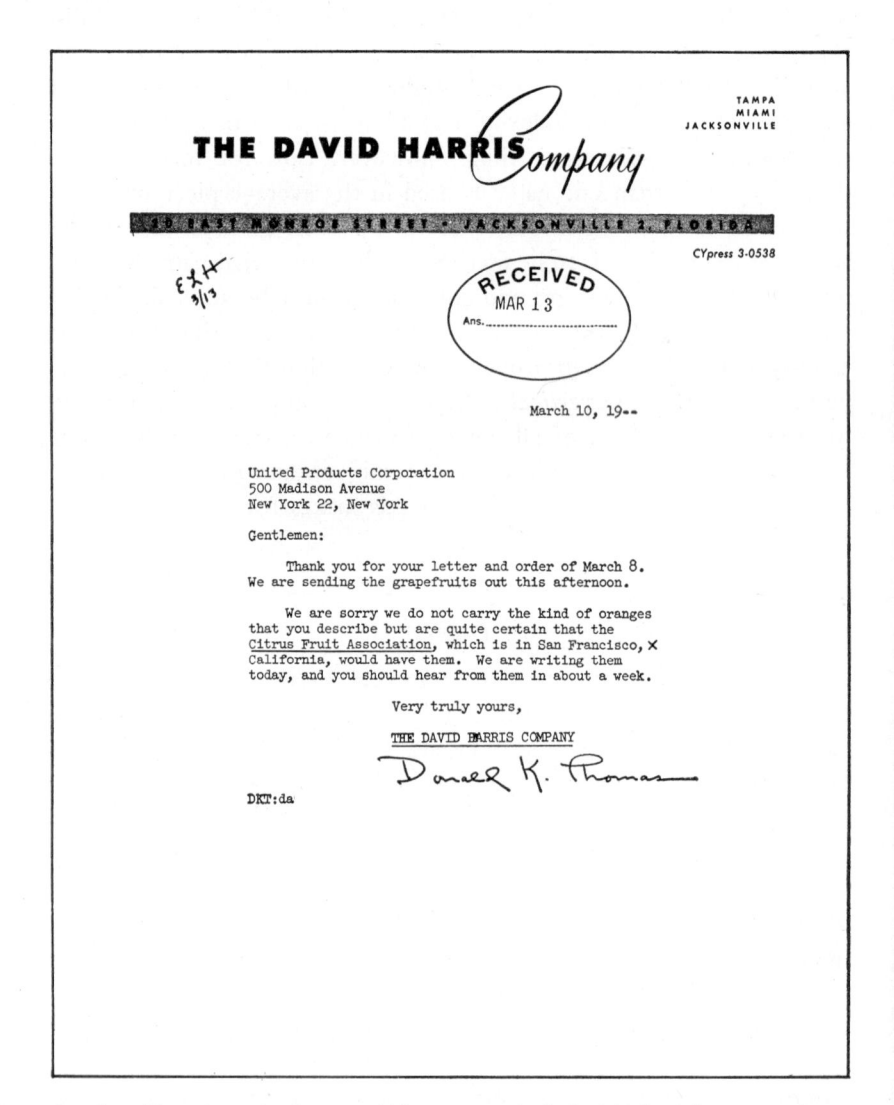

```
                                                            TAMPA
                                                            MIAMI
                                                            JACKSONVILLE
        THE DAVID HARRIS Company

        15 EAST MONROE STREET · JACKSONVILLE 2, FLORIDA
                                                      CYpress 3-0538

                              RECEIVED
          EXH                  MAR 13
          3/13              Ans._____


                                          March 10, 19--

            United Products Corporation
            500 Madison Avenue
            New York 22, New York

            Gentlemen:

                   Thank you for your letter and order of March 8.
            We are sending the grapefruits out this afternoon.

                   We are sorry we do not carry the kind of oranges
            that you describe but are quite certain that the
            Citrus Fruit Association, which is in San Francisco, X
            California, would have them.  We are writing them
            today, and you should hear from them in about a week.

                              Very truly yours,

                              THE DAVID HARRIS COMPANY

                              Donald K. Thomas

            DKT:da
```

The above letter shows the date on which it was received, the initials of the person who released it for filing, as well as the underscoring of the names under which it is to be filed and cross-referenced.

Each person who receives or answers correspondence should have on his desk one or more letter trays. These trays are used for receiving incoming correspondence and for accumulating outgoing letters and material that is ready to be filed. The same tray should *not* be used for both incoming and outgoing material. The best arrangement is one that provides separate containers for each class of material.

A two-tier letter tray for incoming and outgoing mail.

Courtesy Yawman and Erbe Mfg. Co.

Correspondence to be filed should not be permitted to accumulate for a long period but should be collected and filed at *regular* intervals. Material in properly kept files is safe and easy to locate; material in desk trays or drawers is not.

After the interested person has answered or otherwise attended to incoming mail, he marks each piece to show that it has received the required attention. Such marks, known as release marks, may be initials, the date, or both, as illustrated on page 32. They are placed either by hand or by rubber stamp, usually in the upper left corner of the paper. Whatever method is adopted should be used uniformly to tell the person responsible for filing that he has the authority to do so with the piece so marked. It is not necessary to use release marks on carbon copies of outgoing correspondence to indicate readiness for filing, because the carbon copy itself shows that whatever action was required has been taken.

Courtesy National Broadcasting Co.

These girls are coding and sorting correspondence preparatory to filing.

Steps in the Filing Process

There are five steps in the vertical filing of correspondence: (1) inspecting, (2) indexing, (3) coding, (4) sorting, and (5) filing.

Step 1. Inspecting

The first step in preparing correspondence for the file is to *inspect* each piece to make sure that it has been released for filing. Any piece of incoming correspondence not marked for release should be returned to the person who worked with it to obtain authority for the file operator to place it in its proper folder in the file.

Step 2. Indexing

Indexing of correspondence is the process of determining the name, subject, or other caption under which that correspondence is to be filed. There are five possibilities:

1. Under the name on the letterhead
2. Under the name of the person or company to whom the letter is addressed
3. Under the name in the signature
4. Under the name or subject mentioned in the letter
5. Under the name of a location

In selecting an indexing caption, the indexer must determine the most likely heading under which correspondence will be requested from the files.

Whenever a paper might be called for in several ways, it is filed under the most important caption and cross-referenced under the other names or subjects. *Cross-referencing* means placing a sheet of paper containing information about the actual location of a document in all places in a file where a person might look for that document. Cross-reference sheets are usually yellow or some other distinctive color.

A cross-reference sheet

CROSS REFERENCE SHEET

Name or Subject Bicycle Tires   File No.

Regarding Adaptability   Date April 12, 19--

SEE

Name or Subject Automobile Tires   File No.

Center Garage
Detroit, Michigan

File cross reference form under name or subject at top of the sheet and by the latest date of papers. Describe matter for identification purposes. The papers, themselves, should be filed under name or subject after "SEE."

Library Bureau
Division of
Remington Rand Inc.

Cat. No. 30-5902.1
For use in all Filing Systems

36 | PROGRESSIVE FILING

Step 3. Coding

Coding is the process of marking the correspondence with the caption determined upon during the indexing operation. There are three common methods of coding correspondence for alphabetic systems.

1. The name selected to serve as the indexing caption is underlined, usually with a colored pencil. In some large organizations, a different colored pencil is used for coding the papers of each department, to speed finding.
2. If the name or caption under which the letter is to be filed cannot be underlined because it does not appear in the letter, that name is written in colored pencil in the upper right-hand corner.
3. If a letter is to be cross-referenced, the name under which it is actually to be filed is underlined or, if necessary, written. The name under which it is to be cross-referenced is also underlined or written, but in addition an *x* is placed at the end of the line to show that it is not the original filing caption. (See the illustration of a coded letter on page 32.)

Coding not only saves the time of the operator when filing papers for the first time, but also when refiling papers that have been returned after having been used.

Step 4. Sorting

Sorting is the preliminary arrangement of papers according to the caption that has been underlined or written on the paper during the coding process. It is the last step preparatory to the actual filing and arranges the papers in approximate sequence, so that the placing of the papers in the file drawers will be speeded up. Even the smallest office system usually consists of several drawers. Without preliminary arranging, the worker would have to shift back and forth from drawer to drawer while filing the papers, opening and closing the drawers many times, losing time, and wasting energy. Sorting makes it possible to open each drawer only once and to work systematically in each drawer from front to back.

In most organizations where there are many papers to be filed, special equipment is used to speed up the sorting process. If special equipment is not available, the papers to be filed may be sorted on a table or desk top. In this type of sorting, a routine similar to the following should be adopted:

1. Sort the papers into a small number of piles according to convenient divisions. For example, the following groups might be decided upon: *A-C, D-G, H-L, M-R,* and *S-Z.*
2. Take each of the groups used in Step 1 and re-sort the papers into separate piles for each letter of the alphabet. For example, if the first group used in Step 1 was *A-C,* this pile would be redivided into three separate piles, one for *A,* one for *B,* and one for *C.*
3. Arrange, in correct sequence, the papers in each alphabetic letter pile. For example, in the *B* pile, papers to be filed under *Becker* would be placed behind *Baldwin* papers; *Blaine* papers behind *Becker,* etc.
4. Combine all papers to be filed into one or a few alphabetically arranged groups. The number of these final groups will depend on the volume to be filed, the number of file drawers, and other factors peculiar to the filing system used in the specific office.

Step 5. Filing

The fifth step in vertical correspondence filing is the actual *filing* or placing of the papers or records in a file container, usually a folder, according to a predetermined plan. The use of rubber finger tips will add to the speed with which papers can be handled. Papers torn or in bad condition should be repaired with mending tape before being placed in the folder.

The folder should be raised and rested on the side of the drawer before papers are placed within it, to make sure that the correct folder has been selected and to allow papers to be placed evenly and to fall to the bottom of the folder. Lifting the

38 | PROGRESSIVE FILING

A Multisort

The Multisort is a convenient top-of-desk sorter. A sorting tray, sometimes on a stand on wheels, has about the same number of guides as an actual file and therefore helps to speed up the filing process.

A sorting tray

folder and resting it on the side of the drawer also saves time in finding its place again.

After the folder has been found, the caption on it should be checked very carefully with the name underscored on the paper being filed and also with the name coded on the first paper already in the folder. The eye will catch such underscores at a glance and the misfiling of papers will be prevented.

All papers, regardless of size, are placed in folders with the headings to the left as you face the file.

Never overcrowd folders. Standard folders have a maximum capacity of 100 pieces, but it is better to subdivide papers before reaching this capacity. Overcrowding makes the papers "ride up" in the folder and

Scored folders, the last two with tabs

project above the label, or pulls the back of the folder down and hides the label. Every folder should stand on the flat bottom edge. Folders have scores, or creases, across the bottom of the front flap. These scores adjust a folder to the increasing bulk of filed papers, permitting the back flap to remain upright. Do not break scores until the volume in the folder requires it, thus keeping the folder standing upright in the file with the label visible. When the scored capacity is reached, use a second folder.

QUESTIONS

for Review and Discussion

1. What is considered correspondence for filing purposes?
2. What is meant by the term "vertical filing"?
3. What are the advantages of vertical filing?
4. What decisions have to be made in correspondence filing?
5. What is the purpose of vertical correspondence filing?
6. What is meant by stamping time on incoming correspondence? What is its purpose?
7. For what are desk letter trays used?
8. Why should correspondence not be permitted to accumulate too long before being filed?
9. What is the purpose of a release mark? What may be used as release marks?
10. What are the five steps in vertical correspondence filing?
11. What is the purpose of "inspecting" correspondence to be filed?
12. In what ways may correspondence be indexed?
13. What is the general rule for selecting an indexing caption?
14. What is meant by the term "coding"?
15. What are the three methods of coding correspondence?
16. What is meant by the term "sorting"? What is its advantage?
17. Suggest a procedure for use when special sorting equipment is not available.
18. What types of papers require special attention before being placed in folders?
19. What procedure is used to make sure that the papers to be filed will be placed in the correct folder?
20. What is the maximum capacity of a standard folder?
21. What is the danger in overcrowding a folder?
22. What is the purpose of "scoring" folders?
23. What is cross-referencing?

Chapter 4

Alphabetic Correspondence Filing

What Is Alphabetic Filing?

The alphabet, and the correct sequence of letters in it, is used in all systems of filing, inasmuch as names usually provide the captions under which material is filed. In alphabetic systems, the captions are names of people or organizations. In geographic systems, the captions are names of places. In subject systems, the captions are names of objects or categories. In numeric systems, the captions are numbers that have been assigned to names and subjects which are listed alphabetically in an index.

Occasionally, one system will overlap another. For example, in alphabetic systems, a subject title might appear; in geographic systems, a person or organization title; in subject systems, a person or geographic title. Therefore, many of the statements made in this chapter about the procedures and materials of alphabetic filing apply to all methods.

Filing Materials and Their Use

Guides

Guides perform two functions: (1) they act as "signposts" to guide the eye quickly to the places desired in the drawer; (2) they help to support the records contained in the drawer. Guides usually are made of heavy cardboard or pressboard with the "body" slightly larger than the papers to be filed. The projections, or tabs, that extend above the body of the guides are made in various widths, known as *cuts*. When the tab occupies one-fifth of the space on the upper edge, it is called a *one-fifth cut guide*. It is called a *one-third cut guide* when the tab occupies one-third of the space on the upper edge, and a *one-half cut guide* when the tab occupies one-half the space on the upper edge.

The tabs may appear in various places, called *positions*, along the top edge of the guide. These positions are identified by the place in which they occur, reading from left to right. When a tab is one-fifth cut and placed at the extreme left of the upper edge, the guide is termed *one-fifth cut, first position*. When a tab is one-third cut and placed in the center of the upper edge, the guide is termed *one-third cut, center position*. Guides are said to be in *staggered arrangement* when the tabs are in different positions, each position following the previous position, reading from left to right in the file drawer. In the illustrations, the guides are in staggered arrangement.

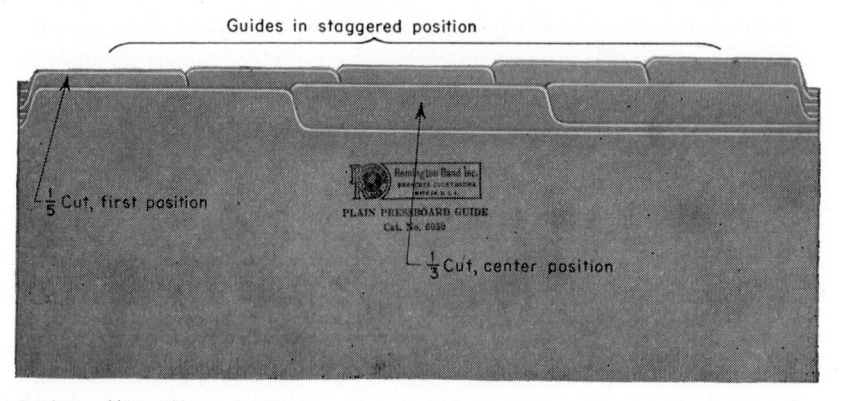

Guides in ⅕ cut, ⅓ cut position

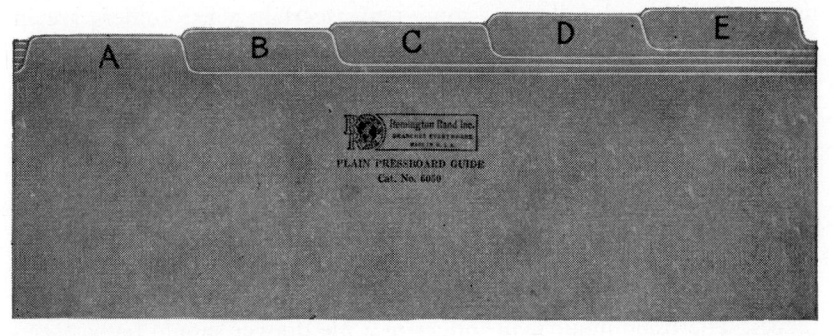

Staggered guides with single captions

Guide Captions

The titles printed on the guide tabs are called *captions* or *notations*. When selecting guide captions, whether they be divisions of the alphabet, names, or subjects, remember to make them short, so that they can be read easily and quickly. The illustration shows guides with single captions. As the name implies, *single caption* means that only one letter or one combination of letters appears on a guide tab. The names to be filed *after* any guide are those beginning with the caption printed on that guide tab and up to, but *not* including, the caption printed on the next guide tab.

Double, or *closed*, captions not only indicate where a section of the file starts but also where it ends. Sometimes double captions are written side by side and separated by a hyphen, as *A-Al, Ale-All;* and sometimes they are written one below the other, as

A	Ale
Al	All

The labels on the drawers of the file cabinet illustrated on page 44 show a double, or closed, caption.

Single captions have the advantage of making expansion easy, because additional guides can be inserted at any place where subdivision is considered advisable. Single captions are also simple to read and often permit larger, more legible letters on the tabs. Double captions have the advantage of showing the entire alphabetic range covered by the guide, whereas with single captions the worker has to look at both the preceding and following guides to ascertain what folders are in between.

A special type of closed caption, known as *multiple caption*, not only shows the beginning and end of the alphabetic section but also the most frequently used part or parts of this section.

The standard vertical file drawer, about 26 inches in depth, has a maximum capacity of 5,000 pieces of paper with the necessary guides and folders. However, this capacity permits little operating space. To insure efficient operation, the maximum number should be about 4,000 pieces. The usual number of guides in a file drawer should be between 20 and 40 in order to provide proper distribution of papers, facilitate reference, and furnish support. The filing needs of the specific office will determine the number of guides used. The guide captions can be

This vertical file cabinet has labels on the drawers showing a double, or closed, caption.

made in the office, or printed alphabetic guides may be purchased. These printed guides are made in various divisions of the alphabet from a set of 10 guides for the very small office up to a set of 200,000 guides for a very large organization.

To protect the guide captions, the guides should be handled as much as possible from the sides, not by the tabs, unless the guides are heavy-weight with strong metal tabs. The life of the guides at the back of the drawer will be prolonged if they are not used to pull forward the papers in the entire drawer. The contents of the drawer should be straightened occasionally by pulling forward the bottoms of the folders at intervals of about 5 inches, starting at the front of the drawer and working to the back.

Folders

In correspondence filing, there are two distinct classes of correspondents and subjects: (1) inactive, and (2) active. Correspondents and subjects are considered to be inactive when fewer than five papers relating to them are received during the filing period, which may be from six months to two years, depending on the needs of the firm. Correspondents and subjects are considered to be active when five or more papers relating to them have been received during the filing period.

In an alphabetic correspondence file drawer, there usually are folders to provide for the two classes of correspondents and subjects: miscellaneous folders for the inactive, and individual folders for the active. Folders, like guides, may be obtained with the caption tabs in various widths and positions.

Miscellaneous Folders

Unless it can be determined at the outset that a correspondent or subject will be active, the first letter from or to this correspondent is placed in the group folder that accompanies each guide in the filing system being used. This group folder usually bears the same caption as the preceding guide and is known as the *miscellaneous* or *alphabetic-tab* folder. It is the temporary housing for correspondence that does not warrant an individual folder. As mentioned before, five pieces

46 | PROGRESSIVE FILING

pertaining to one name or subject usually are permitted to accumulate in this miscellaneous folder before an individual folder is assigned to it.

This miscellaneous folder contains papers pertaining to a variety of names, since it is the depository for all inactive correspondents. These names are arranged in alphabetic sequence. Where two or more papers pertain to the same name, these papers are arranged in order by date, with the latest date on top. Related papers should be fastened together in the upper right-hand corner. Staples are preferred to paper clips or pins, because they are less likely to slip and are less bulky and dangerous. If subsequent papers are added to the papers previously stapled, use a second staple without removing the first. As many as four staples may be used without adding bulk.

Individual Folders

When five or more papers have accumulated about one correspondent or subject, an individual folder is made. This is done by placing the name of the correspondent or subject on the caption tab of a folder.

An individual folder will contain correspondence about only one name or one subject. This correspondence will include both original incoming papers and carbon copies of outgoing papers. Usually when a paper is wanted from the files, the date as well as the name is given. Consequently, it is most convenient to have all papers within an individual folder arranged according to date, with the latest date on top. The most recent papers are placed on top because they are the ones most likely to be requested from the files. In some special situations, papers in an individual folder might be called for by location or by subject as well as by name. In such cases, papers should *not* be arranged by date but in an order that permits the fastest and easiest location.

Individual folders must not be allowed to become too bulky for convenient handling. Standard-sized folders will hold 100 sheets of paper and stand up. Beyond 100 sheets, the folder curls down in the drawer and the tabs become hidden or invisible. When correspondence nears this volume, it should be separated either by date, or by location, or by subject.

Preparation of Folder Labels

Captions may be typed directly on the folder tabs or on separate gummed labels. The labels, about 4 inches wide, may be purchased in perforated strips or in continuous rolls. In either form, they are obtainable in a variety of colors. Remember the following suggestions and illustrations when typing folder labels:

1. Labels have a front and a back portion with a crease between. The wider section, if either is wider, is always the front of the label. Start the caption on the third space from the left edge of the front portion and on the second line below the crease. The caption should be started at the same place on every folder label, so that, when looking from the front to the rear of a file drawer, all first words will be in a straight line. This makes the reading of captions easier and facilitates finding.
2. The words or items of the caption are typed in indexing order.
3. In some offices, the entire first line of a label is capitalized; in others, only the first letter of each important word is capitalized. The latter style is preferred; however, whichever style is adopted should be used consistently on all labels.
4. In some offices, punctuation, including the period after abbreviations, is omitted entirely. Instead, two spaces are left where the punctuation would have been. Other offices use normal punctuation. Whatever method is used should be used consistently. Both styles are shown in this book.
5. Block style is preferred if the caption includes more than one item. If any line in the caption runs over to a second line, the runover should be indented three spaces.

```
    Northern States Gas Electric
       (&) Power Company     1955
```
Alphabetic label with year notations

```
    Accounting Systems
    Provision for Depreciation
```
Subject label

```
    Detroit  Mich
    Western Electric Company
```
Geographic label

```
    28-463-705
```
Numeric label

The following suggestions will help in attaching the typed labels to the folder tabs:

1. After typing the strip of labels, obtain a desk sponge, two blotters, and a pencil.

2. For easier separation, fold the labels on the perforations before tearing.

3. Draw the label across the sponge while pressing with the pencil to assure even moistening.

4. Moisten the other end of the label in a similar manner.

5. Place the label, *gummed side up*, on a blotter.

6. Lay the folder tab on the label with the top edge of the tab at the center of the label along the folding score. The label should be close to the left edge of the folder tab, or centered on the tab, if the label is nearly as wide as the tab.

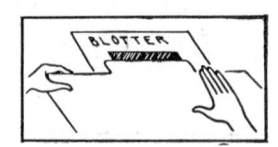

7. Slip the second blotter under the projecting half of the label.

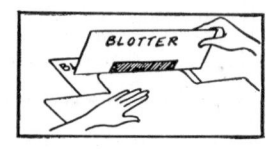

8. Move the blotter toward you while pressing the label down on the front of the tab.

Arrangement of Guides and Folders in the Drawer

Individual folders are arranged in alphabetic order *after* each guide. At the *end* of the group of individual folders, behind any one guide, there should be a miscellaneous folder bearing the same caption as the guide controlling the group.

When filing papers, the worker locates the correct guide, looks over the individual folders following the guide, and, if there is no individual folder for that name or subject, places the correspondence in the only remaining folder in the group—the miscellaneous folder. Thus, placing the miscellaneous folder after the individual folders prevents filing errors and prevents lost effort, because the operating motion is always forward. Were the miscellaneous folders to be placed before the individual folders in each section, the worker might make the mistake of filing papers in the miscellaneous folder without first trying to find an individual folder; or, having checked the individual folders and not finding one, the worker would then have to move back to place papers in the miscellaneous folder before moving forward again to the next group.

The number of individual folders filed behind any one guide should average five to ten. If the file drawer is entirely miscellaneous, the average number of miscellaneous folders behind any one guide should be five.

Filing Cabinets

Each drawer of a filing cabinet should be plainly marked to identify the contents. Printed or typewritten labels inserted in the holder on the front will assist in locating the correct drawer rapidly.

When more than one loaded drawer of a cabinet is pulled out at one time, there is a possibility of the cabinet's becoming top-heavy and toppling over on the worker. As a precaution, it is advisable to adopt the practice of shutting one drawer before opening another. Securing filing cabinets together or to the floor will have the double advantage of eliminating toppling as well as the creeping that sometimes takes place on smooth floors.

Open file drawers can be the cause of bad falls or cuts for anyone

50 | PROGRESSIVE FILING

unaware of their being open. To avoid such accidents, every person working with files should be sure he has closed every drawer all the way when he has completed his work.

Courtesy Globe-Wernicke Co.

A well-arranged alphabetic correspondence file with uncrowded, clearly labeled drawers

Commercial Alphabetic Systems

Anyone who understands the general principles of alphabetic correspondence filing can probably organize a system to meet the needs of a specific business office. Very often this is what happens: The secretary purchases a quantity of guides and folders from the nearest stationery store and proceeds to set up her own filing plan. There are, however, various patented systems that have already been designed by manufacturers of filing equipment and supplies. These commercial systems are based on the general principles of alphabetic correspondence filing and are easily adaptable to any need.

In keeping with their simplicity, the commercial systems limit the guides to a few easily read positions, so that the folders are more visible. These systems have various features that speed up the filing and finding of material and provide a double check against misfiling, such as: (1) adding corresponding color schemes to guide and folder tabs, (2) combining alphabetic and numeric coded captions, (3) providing for special tab-position sections to take care of frequently used names.

Although the commercial systems differ from one another in the arrangement of guides and folders and in certain special features, they all include the following basic elements: (1) primary guides; (2) special guides, also known as secondary or auxiliary guides; (3) individual folders; (4) miscellaneous folders. A *primary* guide is the main guide and always precedes the special guides, individual folders, and miscellaneous folders that are within the alphabetic range covered by the primary guide. Sets of primary guides may be obtained with subdivisions of the alphabet from 25 up into the thousands. As the name implies, a *special* guide is used to show the location of materials of a special nature that fall within the alphabetic range of the preceding primary guide.

Many patented systems are available from the manufacturers of filing equipment and supplies. A few are described on the following pages to illustrate some of the special features and possible guide and folder arrangements available to facilitate filing.

52 | PROGRESSIVE FILING

Variadex System (manufactured by Remington Rand)
1. Primary guides use single captions and are placed in first position.[1]
2. Special guides are in fourth position for names having a large volume of correspondence.
3. Individual folders are in third position.
4. Miscellaneous folders are in second position and in *back* of the individual folders. They bear the same alphabetic caption as the primary guide.
5. Special features: color is used on the guide tabs and on the folder tabs to speed up the location of papers and as a check to prevent misfiling. The color of all folder tabs behind a guide is the same as the color of that guide tab. A worker would, therefore, be aware that he was misfiling if he tried to place a folder with a *green* tab with folders having *blue* tabs.

The colors, in rainbow sequence, are based on the following divisions of the alphabet into five sections:

If the SECOND letter of the first unit of the name is:	The color on the guide and folder tabs for that section will be:	Examples
a, b, c, or d	orange	Baker
e, f, g, or h	yellow	Bennett
i, j, k, l, m, or n	green	Binney
o, p, or q	blue	Bond
r, s, t, u, v, w, x, y, or z	violet	Brattle

When there is no second letter in the first unit of a guide caption or in a folder name, as in the name *A and B Company*, orange is used.

The second letter of the first unit in the name is used as the basis for determining color rather than the first letter of the first unit, because research has shown that 78 per cent of the second letters are vowels; and these vowels divide a file approximately into five equal parts.

The color orange would be used for the name *Acme Tire Company* because *Acme* is the first indexing unit and the letter *c* is the second letter of that first unit. The color violet would be used for the name

---

[1] "Position," as used in the description of the commercial systems, refers to the order of the tabs as seen from left to right. It does not necessarily refer to the location of the tab according to its cut size as described on page 42.

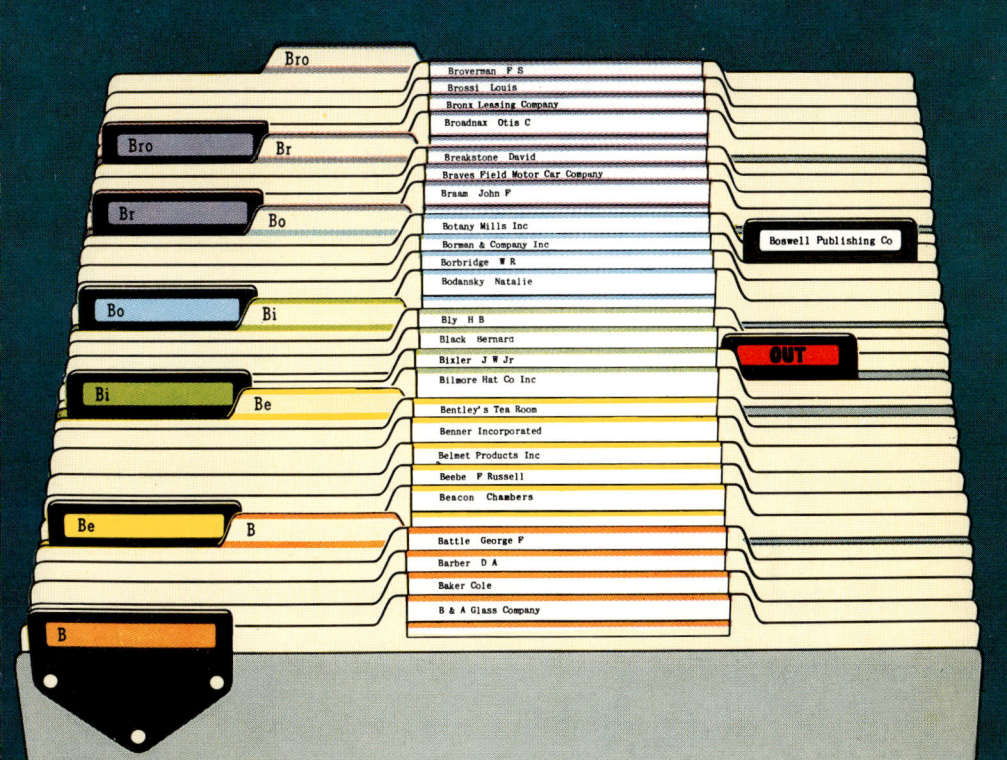

Bro			
	Broverman F S		
	Brossi Louis		
	Bronx Leasing Company		
	Broadnax Otis C		

Bro	Br		
	Breakstone David		
	Braves Field Motor Car Company		
	Braam John F		

Br	Bo		
	Botany Mills Inc		
	Borman & Company Inc	Boswell Publishing Co	
	Borbridge W R		
	Bodansky Natalie		

Bo	Bi		
	Bly H B		
	Black Bernard	OUT	
	Bixler J W Jr		
	Bilmore Hat Co Inc		

Bi	Be		
	Bentley's Tea Room		
	Benner Incorporated		
	Belmet Products Inc		
	Beebe F Russell		
	Beacon Chambers		

Be	B		
	Battle George F		
	Barber D A		
	Baker Cole		
	B & A Glass Company		

B

PRODUCT OF
Remington Rand
MADE IN U.S.A.

LIBRARY BUREAU DEPARTMENT
BRANCHES EVERYWHERE

VARIADEX
U. S. PATENT NO. 1929383
ARMORCLAD
GUIDES AND FOLDERS

IN ORDERING GIVE CAT.
NO. 602.—ALSO NUMBER
OF DIVISIONS.

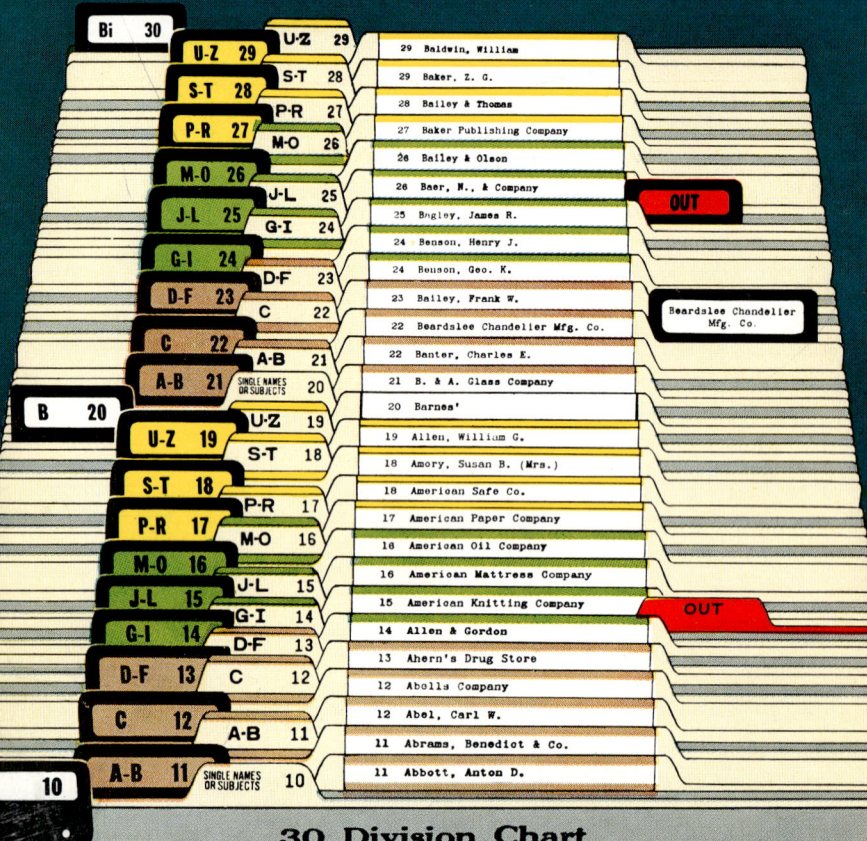

Tab	Entry
Bi 30	
U-Z 29	29 Baldwin, William
S-T 28	29 Baker, Z. G.
P-R 27	28 Bailey & Thomas
M-O 26	27 Baker Publishing Company
J-L 25	26 Bailey & Olson
G-I 24	26 Baer, N. & Company
D-F 23	25 Bagley, James R.
C 22	24 Benson, Henry J.
A-B 21	24 Benson, Geo. K.
SINGLE NAMES OR SUBJECTS 20	23 Bailey, Frank W.
B 20	22 Beardslee Chandelier Mfg. Co.
U-Z 19	22 Banter, Charles E.
S-T 18	21 B. & A. Glass Company
P-R 17	20 Barnes'
M-O 16	19 Allen, William G.
J-L 15	18 Amory, Susan B. (Mrs.)
G-I 14	18 American Safe Co.
D-F 13	17 American Paper Company
C 12	16 American Oil Company
A-B 11	16 American Mattress Company
A 10	15 American Knitting Company
	14 Allen & Gordon
	13 Ahern's Drug Store
	12 Abells Company
	12 Abel, Carl W.
	11 Abrams, Benedict & Co.
	11 Abbott, Anton D.

OUT — Beardslee Chandelier Mfg. Co.
OUT

30 Division Chart

A	1	C	5	F	9	I-J	13	M	16	N	19	S	23	U-V	27
B	2	Co	6	G	10	K	14	Mc	17	O	20	Sl	24	W	28
Bi	3	D	7	H	11	L	15	Mo	18	P-Q	21	St	25	Wi	29
Br	4	E	8	Ho	12					R	22	T	26	XYZ	30

For subdivision of these sections see the guides following.

TRIPLE AUTOMATIC "Armorclad"
Guides and Folders
Remington Rand Inc.
IN ORDERING GIVE CATALOG NO. 60611
ALSO NO. OF DIVISIONS

ALPHABETIC CORRESPONDENCE FILING | 53

James Irwin because *Irwin* is the first indexing unit and the letter *r* is the second letter of that first unit.

The miscellaneous folders in second position are colored to match the guides to which they correspond and are filed behind the individual folders.

Triple-Check Automatic Index (manufactured by Remington Rand)
1. Primary guides use single captions and are placed in first position.
2. Special guides are of two types: those that are alphabetical subdivisions are placed in the second position; those that are common names or subjects are placed in the fifth position.
3. Individual folders are in the fourth position.
4. Miscellaneous folders are in third position and in *back* of the individual folders.
5. Special features: the use of section numbers to increase speed and accuracy. A uniform set of special alphabetic subdivision guides, nine in number, follows each primary guide. The primary guides are numbered according to a primary number chart, shown on the illustration on the facing page. The primary charts vary according to the number of guides in the set purchased, but the special alphabetic subdivisions are always the same, whether they follow *A* or *B* or any other letter of the alphabet. These subdivisions are numbered as follows: A-B 1; C 2; D-F 3; G-I 4; J-L 5; M-O 6; P-R 7; S-T 8; U-Z 9. Each number is preceded by the first digit of the primary guide. Thus, if the primary guide is 20 for *B* section, the first subdivision would be 21, while under *A* it would be 11.

The illustration lists the numbers for the primary guides, omitting the zero for each. On the chart, *A* is listed as 1, but the primary guide caption would actually be 10; *Bi* is listed as 3 on the chart, but the *Bi* guide would bear the number 30.

The primary guides are used exactly the same as the alphabetic guides in any alphabetic system of filing; that is, to locate the *first* indexing unit of the name or subject. The special alphabetic guides, however, are used to subdivide papers filed after the primary guide according to the *second* indexing unit of the name. Correspondence that is to be filed under this system is coded by its location number as well as by underlining or writing the name.

54 | PROGRESSIVE FILING

Example 1 Correspondence pertaining to *Carl W. Abel* is coded *12* (*10* from the primary chart for the letter *A* of *Abel*, the first indexing unit, plus *2* from the subdivision chart for the letter *C* of *Carl*, the second unit). It would be filed behind the *A-10* primary guide and behind the *C-12* subdivision guide either in an individual folder labeled *12 Abel, Carl W.* or, if he was not active enough for an individual folder, in the *C-12* miscellaneous folder.

Example 2 Correspondence pertaining to the *Baker Stationery Company* is coded *28*. (*20* from the primary chart for the letter *B* of *Baker*, the first indexing unit, plus *8* from the subdivision chart for the letter *S* of *Stationery*, the second unit.) It would be filed behind the *B-20* primary guide and behind the *S-T 28* subdivision guide either in an individual folder labeled *28 Baker Stationery Company* or, if it is not active enough for an individual folder, in the *S-T 28* miscellaneous folder.

Example 3 Correspondence pertaining to a company with the single name of *Barnes'* is coded *20*. (*20* from the primary chart for the letter *B* of *Barnes'*, the first indexing unit, plus *zero* because there is no second unit.) It would be filed behind the *B-20* primary guide either in an individual folder labeled *20 Barnes'* or, if it is not active enough for an individual folder, in the miscellaneous folder labeled *Single Name or Subject*.

Color is also used to assist in identifying guides and labels. The tabs of the first three special alphabetic subdivision guides in each section are tan; the second three in each section are green, and the last three in each section are yellow. The labels on the individual folders and miscellaneous folders are colored to match the special subdivision guides they follow. The tabs of the primary guides are plain white, and the labels on the individual folders and miscellaneous folders immediately after them are plain Manila without a special color.

Amberg "Nual" Alphabet Index (manufactured by Amberg File & Index Company)

1. Primary guides use double captions and are staggered in second, third, and fourth positions.
2. Special guides, called "Leader Equipment" in this system, are in the first position.
3. Individual folders are staggered in approximately second, third, and fourth positions.
4. Miscellaneous folders are in first position and in *front* of the individual folders.
5. Special features: the use of section numbers to speed up filing and finding and as a safeguard against misfiling. The primary guides are numbered consecutively. All special guides, individual folders, and the miscellaneous folder bear the same number as the primary guide they follow.

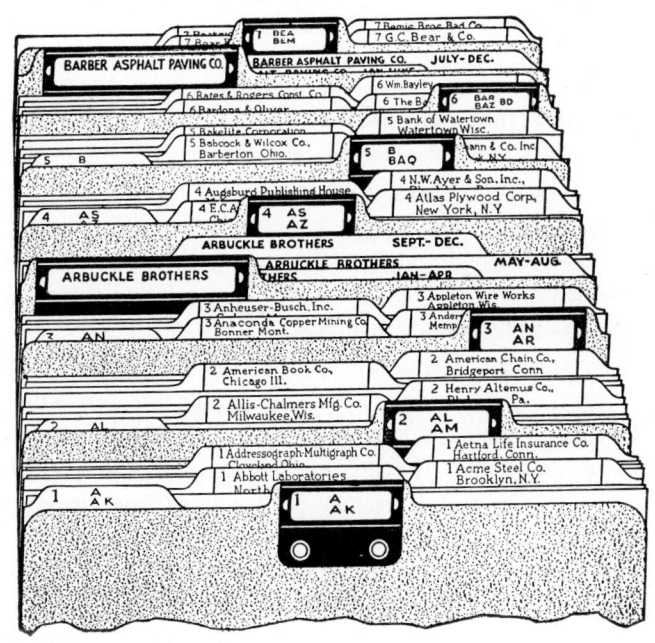

Amberg "Nual" alphabet index

F. E. Bee Line Filing System (manufactured by the Filing Equipment Bureau)
1. Primary guides use single captions and are placed in the first position.
2. Special guides are in fourth position.
3. Individual folders are in third position.
4. Miscellaneous folders are in second position and in *back* of the individual folders.
5. Special features: the use of section numbers to speed up filing and finding and as a safeguard against misfiling. The primary guides are numbered consecutively. All special guides, individual folders, and the miscellaneous folder bear the same number as the primary guide they follow. Color is used to aid in identification—the tabs of miscellaneous folders are salmon colored, while the individual folders are obtainable with tabs of various colors that can be used to distinguish the folders in any way that lends itself best to the needs of the particular office.

"Safeguard" Index (manufactured by Globe-Wernicke)
1. Primary guides use single captions and are staggered in the first, second, and third positions.
2. Special guides are in fourth position.
3. Individual folders are in fifth position.
4. Miscellaneous folders are in first, second, and third positions and in *back* of the individual folders.
5. Special features: the use of section numbers to increase speed and accuracy. The primary guides are numbered consecutively. All special guides, individual folders, and the miscellaneous folder bear the same number as the primary guide they follow. Color is used to guide the eye. All primary guides are green, and all miscellaneous folders are red. Various colored labels can be fastened to individual folder tabs to differentiate between correspondents in the same classification. Because the miscellaneous folders are in the same positions as the primary guides, the primary guide tabs are made more conspicuous by having the miscellaneous folder tabs stand a little lower.

F. E. Bee Line filing system

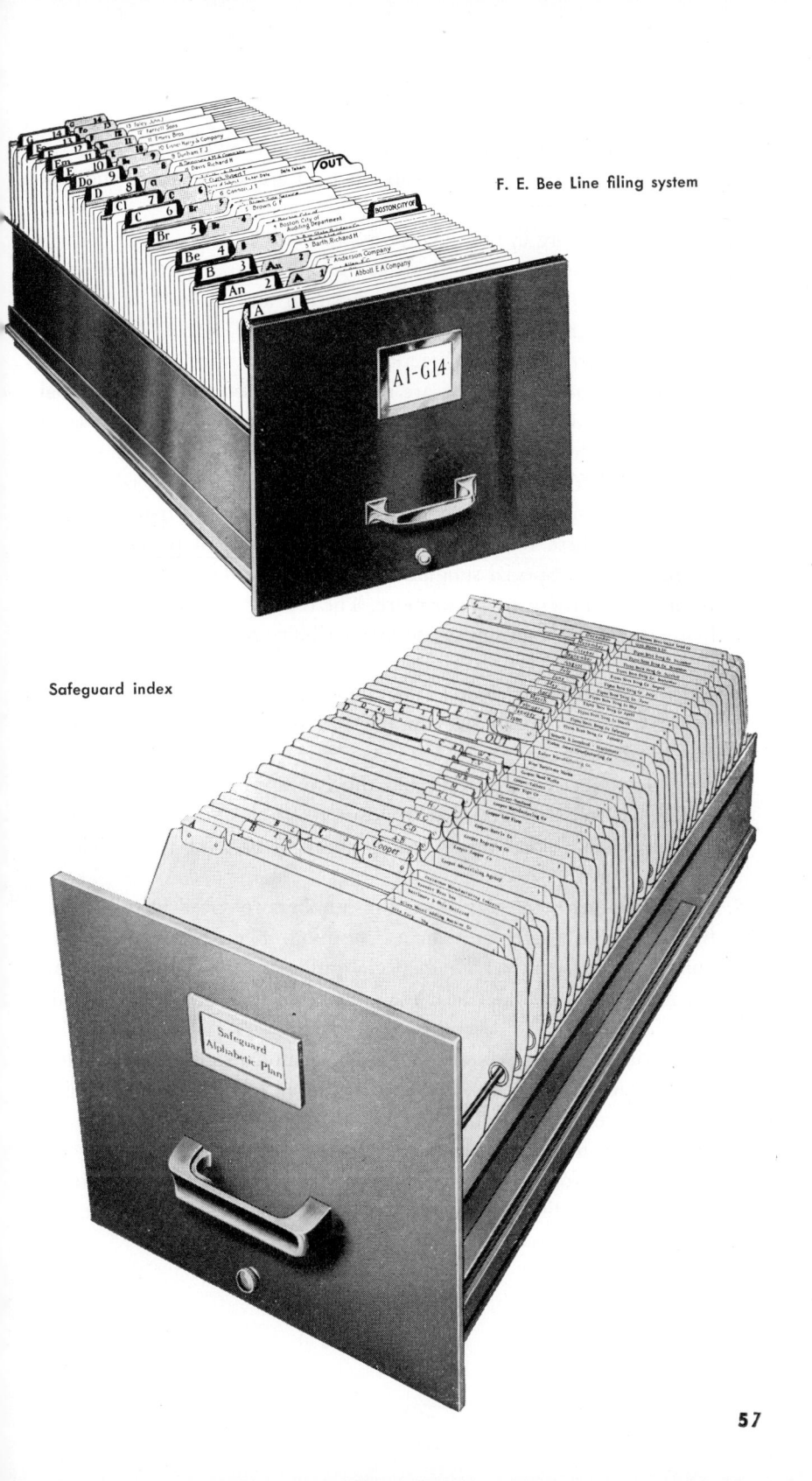

Safeguard index

"Tailor-Made" Index (manufactured by Shaw-Walker)
1. Primary guides use multiple captions and are staggered in the first and second positions.
2. Special guides are in the third position.
3. Individual folders are staggered in the second and third position.
4. Miscellaneous folders are in first position and in *back* of the individual folders.
5. Special features: the use of section numbers as a speed and accuracy device. The primary guides are numbered consecutively. All special guides, individual folders, and the miscellaneous folder bear the same number as the primary guide they follow. Not only are special guides used for very active firms or individuals, but special folders are used to subdivide their correspondence by time periods. The number of these folders depends on the volume of papers for the correspondent. Special subguides are used to index the time-period folders when there are six or more. The top edge of all folders is just below the guide captions to increase visibility for the guide captions.

Y and E "Direct-Name" Index (manufactured by Yawman and Erbe)
1. Primary guides use double captions and are staggered in the second and third positions.
2. Special guides are in second and third positions.
3. Individual folders are in fourth position.
4. Miscellaneous folders are in first position in *back* of the individual folders.
5. Special features: the use of section numbers to speed up filing and finding and as a safeguard against misfiling. The primary guides are numbered consecutively. All special guides, individual folders, and the miscellaneous folder bear the same number as the primary guide they follow.

In primary guide sets of more than 40 subdivisions, the first division of each letter of the alphabet is printed in red. All other guide headings are printed in black. The miscellaneous-folder captions are also printed in red.

Individual folders can be obtained with an extended tab to be used in subdividing by time period the papers of very active correspondents.

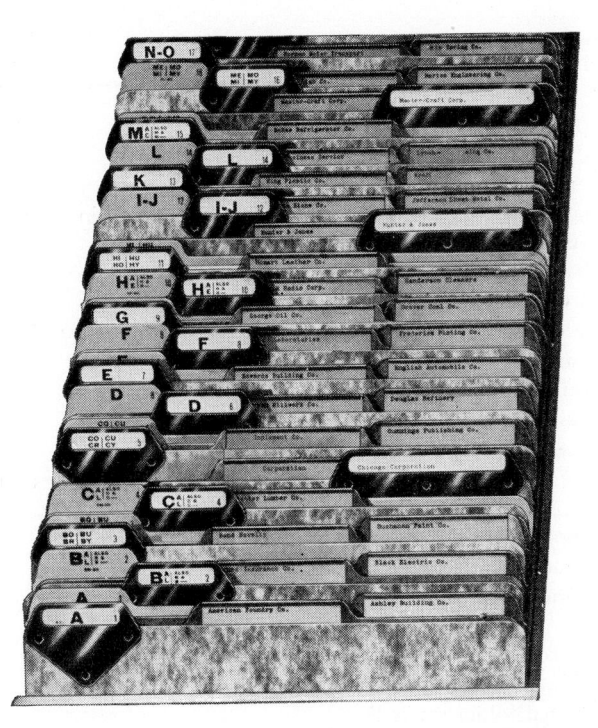

"Tailor-Made" index

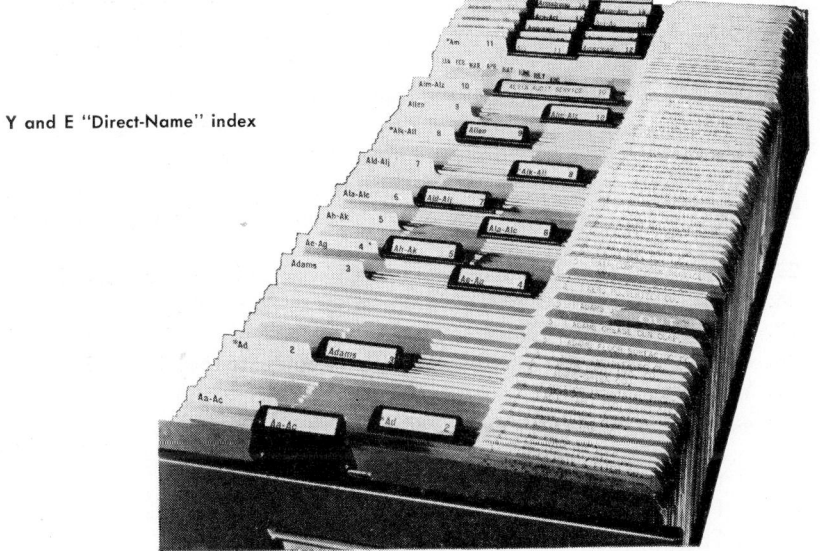

Y and E "Direct-Name" index

QUESTIONS

for Review and Discussion

1. What is used in all methods of filing?
2. What are, primarily, the captions in an alphabetic system? in a geographic system? in a subject system? in a numeric system?
3. What is meant by the terms "cut," "position," and "staggered arrangement" as applied to filing guides?
4. What are "single captions"? "double captions"?
5. What is a disadvantage of double captions?
6. What is the maximum capacity of a standard vertical file drawer?
7. What is the working capacity of a standard vertical file drawer?
8. How many guides ordinarily are used in a file drawer?
9. What can be done to prolong the life of the guides and the captions on the guides?
10. When are correspondents or subjects considered to be inactive?
11. When are correspondents or subjects considered to be active?
12. What is a miscellaneous folder?
13. How are papers arranged in a miscellaneous folder?
14. What is the preferred method of fastening related papers together?
15. What is an individual folder?
16. When is an individual folder started?
17. How are papers arranged in an individual folder?
18. What should be the arrangement of folders and guides in a file drawer?
19. What should be the average number of folders filed behind any one guide?
20. Where are captions placed on a folder label?
21. What style is preferred if a folder caption requires more than one line?
22. Describe a procedure for attaching labels to folder tabs.
23. What safety precautions should be adopted with regard to file drawers?
24. How have commercial systems improved alphabetic correspondence filing?
25. What basic elements do all commercial systems have in common?
26. How do commercial systems differ from one another?
27. What is a primary guide?
28. What is a special guide? By what other names are they known?
29. Variadex system:
    a. What type of caption is used on the tabs?
    b. From left to right, what is the arrangement of the guides? of the folders?
    c. From front to back, what is the arrangement of guides and folders?
    d. How is color used?

ALPHABETIC CORRESPONDENCE FILING | 61

30. Triple-Check Automatic Index:
  a. What type of caption is used on the tabs?
  b. From left to right, what is the arrangement of the guides? of the folders?
  c. From front to back, what is the arrangement of guides and folders?
  d. How are numbers used?
  e. How is color used?
31. Amberg "Nual" Index:
  a. What type of caption is used on the tabs?
  b. From left to right, what is the arrangement of the guides? of the folders?
  c. From front to back, what is the arrangement of guides and folders?
  d. How are numbers used?
32. F. E. Bee Line Filing System:
  a. What type of caption is used on the tabs?
  b. From left to right, what is the arrangement of the guides? of the folders?
  c. From front to back, what is the arrangement of guides and folders?
  d. How are numbers used?
  e. How is color used?
33. Safeguard Index:
  a. What type of caption is used on the tabs?
  b. From left to right, what is the arrangement of the guides? of the folders?
  c. From front to back, what is the arrangement of guides and folders?
  d. How are numbers used?
  e. How is color used?
  f. Are the tabs of the folders and guides the same height?
34. Tailor-Made Index:
  a. What type of caption is used on the tabs?
  b. From left to right, what is the arrangement of the guides? of the folders?
  c. From front to back, what is the arrangement of guides and folders?
  d. How are numbers used?
  e. How are individual folders further subdivided?
  f. Are the tabs of the folders and guides the same height?
35. Y and E "Direct-Name" Index:
  a. What type of caption is used on the tabs?
  b. From left to right, what is the arrangement of the guides? of the folders?
  c. From front to back, what is the arrangement of guides and folders?
  d. How are numbers used?
  e. How is color used?
  f. How are individual folders further subdivided?

Chapter 5

Charge Methods

The Need for Control

Material is filed because it is believed the information so collected will be of value in the future. The basic purpose of all filing operations is to produce these desired records in minimum time. There are two principal reasons for delay in obtaining documents from the files.

They might have been misfiled; however, proper application of the basic indexing and filing rules, adequate cross-referencing, and care in placing the correspondence in the correct folder will prevent that.

Or, they may have been removed from the files for use by someone in the organization. Good records management, therefore, goes beyond the original filing and calls for a system of control, so that all material can be accounted for whether it is in the files or in use. Such a system, whether for a large or small organization, should indicate what material is out, who has it, when it was borrowed, and when it will be returned.

CHARGE METHODS | 63

There are three steps in any control, or "charge," system:

1. Handling the request calling for filed material
2. Charging the material against the person or persons calling for it
3. Following up the material until it is returned to the files

The size of the organization will determine the amount of clerical detail in these steps. Obviously the system will be more formal in a large organization, because there is not always direct contact with the people calling for the filed material, the records are used by more people, and the records are spread over a wider area.

Handling Requests for Filed Material

In a large office, the material may be called for in several ways: by telephone, by messenger, or by the personal appearance of the one desiring it. It is advisable to have the requests made in writing on a standard form, whenever possible. Any oral requests should be recorded as soon as they are received on one of the standard requisition forms. These requisition slips may be printed, duplicated, or purchased and should contain the following information:

1. Name or subject of material
2. Date of material
3. Signature or name of borrower
4. Date borrowed
5. Date on which material is to be "followed up" to secure its return

Wherever possible, the requisition should contain the borrower's signature rather than just his name. The signature provides more definite proof of "who has what." The illustration of a tickler file on page 64 shows a requisition card.

In a small office where requests are usually received orally or where the borrower himself obtains the material from the file, the use of a requisition slip is unnecessary if the papers are restored to the files immediately. However, if the material is not to be returned at once, then a requisition slip should be made out, because it is the basis for the second step in a control system "charging the borrower to make him responsible for the return of the material."

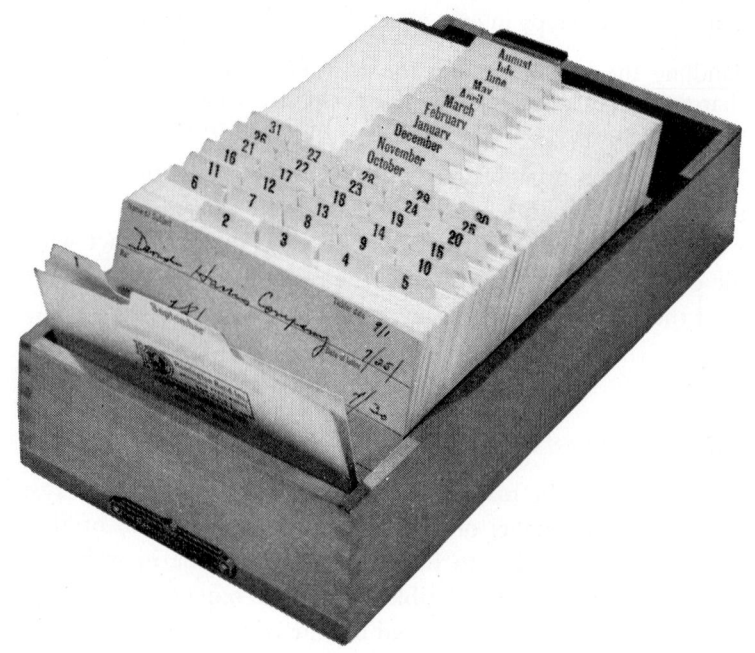

A tickler file showing a requisition card

Charging the Material

When the material requested is removed from the files and sent to the borrower, a notation should be made in the exact filing location. This notation will indicate who has the material. There are three common methods of making such notations: by out guides, by out folders, or by substitution cards. *Substitution cards* are used when individual papers are borrowed from a folder, while *out folders* and *out guides* are used when an entire folder is removed.

Out guides are made of the same heavy cardboard used for the filing location guides. Two types may be obtained: either like number 1 in the illustration on page 65 that has a pocket at the front for the requisition slip or a cumulative style. Both types have advantages—the pocket type eliminates the need for transferring the information on the requisition slip, while the cumulative type provides a history of how the material has been used and by whom.

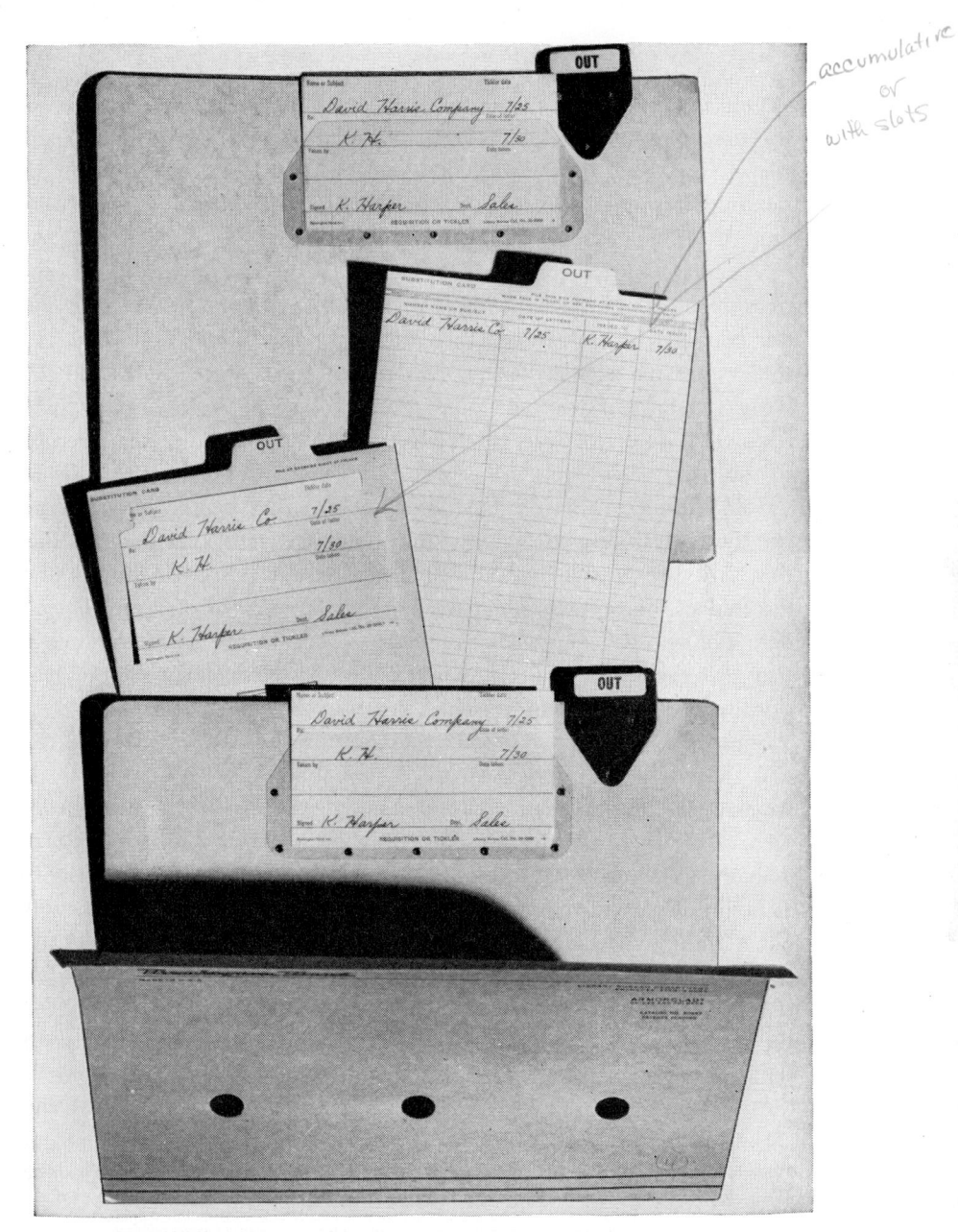

From top to bottom: out guide with requisition card in a pocket; cumulative substitution card; substitution card with requisition card in a pocket; out folder with requisition card in a pocket

65

Out folders are preferred to out guides by many people, because the use of an out folder provides a storage place for any new papers that arrive while the original folder is out of the file. The front of an out folder contains a place for information similar to that written on a cumulative out guide.

When the entire contents of a folder are needed, many file executives recommend that the original folder remain in the drawer and the contents be transferred to a special *carrier* folder. These special folders are made of a heavier material that can better withstand the wear and tear of transportation. Furthermore, they are usually of a distinctive color in order to reduce loss and to expedite their return to the files.

Substitution cards, like out guides, may either be the pocket type for the requisition slip or the cumulative type. However the substitution cards are of a distinctive color and are smaller so that they can be inserted in the regular folder to indicate the removal of a specific paper. The substitution cards should be placed in the folder in such a way that the out tab will show in the position reserved for such indication in the filing system in use.

Sometimes in a large organization, material is requested from the files that is to be referred to the attention of a series of people or departments. Rather than have the material returned to the file department after each person has finished with it for recharging and redelivery, two possible timesaving methods may be used. Each person, as he finishes using the material, passes it on to the next person but fills out a transfer slip that is sent to the file department and used as the basis for recharging the out guide. Or, a list of all persons to use the material is attached to it and each person checks off his name on the list as he passes the material on. A duplicate copy of the list is kept with the out guide, so the material can be traced if necessary.

When material has been returned to its proper place in the files, the substitution card, out guide, or out folder should be removed and the charge-out notation on it marked off, so the borrower is no longer charged with responsibility.

A supply of substitution cards, out guides, or out folders should be kept in the front or back of every file drawer so that they are available for convenient use.

Following up Borrowed Material

The kind of business and the nature of the material will determine how long it may be borrowed. Very confidential or valuable material should be returned to the files every night. Other records may be kept for the period of time set as the standard loan period by the executives of the specific business. A definite time should be set aside to check charge-outs and to trace papers that have been out longer than the allowed loan period. The longer material is allowed to lie around in places other than the files, the more difficult it is to locate. Systematic follow-up will reduce possibilities of loss.

If the organization is small, it is a simple matter for the person responsible for the files to check the due dates of borrowed materials from the substitution cards, out guides, or out folders in the file drawers. When the organization is large, however, too many file drawers would have to be checked, so the follow-up procedure is usually simplified by the use of a desk card follow-up or *tickler* file. See page 64.

In such a system, when material is charged out and a requisition card is inserted in the pocket of an out guide or attached to the substitution card, a duplicate copy of the requisition card is placed in the tickler behind the date on which the borrowed material is to be returned.

Regardless of the follow-up system used, the person responsible for the files checks each day to determine what materials are due and notifies the borrower. If the borrower still needs the material, the due date on the requisition card is extended; otherwise, the materials are returned and the charge canceled.

Sometimes the file department receives a request for filed material to be delivered at some future date. Such requests can be placed behind the proper date in a tickler file. Although one tickler file could be used for both purposes, it is better to have separate ticklers for follow-up purposes and for premature requests.

Despite all precautions, papers do occasionally get lost. As soon as the loss is discovered, as much as possible of the original information should be listed on a specially colored sheet. In this way, subsequent requesters of the lost material will not be kept waiting while the missing material is searched for needlessly or while the information is obtained elsewhere.

PROGRESSIVE FILING

A control system will not function properly unless everyone follows the charge procedures adopted. If people other than those in the filing department have access to the files, they, too, must be required to charge to themselves all material they remove. Even "top executives" must be made to account for their withdrawals if "file leaks that lead to file losses" are not to develop.

QUESTIONS

for Review and Discussion

1. What are the principal reasons for delay in obtaining material from the files?
2. Why is a control system necessary?
3. What are the steps in a control system?
4. Is a control system necessary in a small office?
5. Why must a control system be more formal in a large organization?
6. In what ways may material be requested from the files in a large organization?
7. What information should a file requisition slip contain?
8. Why should a requisition slip contain the borrower's signature, if possible?
9. What are the common forms used for "charging out" filed materials?
10. When are substitution cards used? out guides? out folders?
11. What are the advantages of each type of out guide?
12. Why is the out folder sometimes preferred to the out guide?
13. What is a carrier folder and why is it used?
14. How may charged papers be transferred to another person without returning them to the files?
15. What is done after charged material is returned to the files?
16. What determines how long material may be borrowed from the files?
17. Why should material not be allowed to remain out of the files too long?
18. Describe a follow-up procedure that may be used in a small organization; in a large organization.
19. Describe a procedure that can be used when a request is received for material to be delivered on some future date.
20. What should be done when it is definitely discovered that material has been lost?
21. What must be done if a control system is to function properly?

Chapter 6

Transfer Methods

Need for Transfer

Business organizations are faced with the problem of what records to keep and where to keep them. Three factors should be considered in arriving at decisions: will the material be used, and if so, how often, and for how long.

The amount of office space that can be devoted to filing cabinets obviously must be limited to allow room for other operations of the business. Because the easily accessible filing cabinets should be reserved for records that are used frequently, they are called *active* files. As this valuable space fills up, provision should be made to transfer the lesser-used materials to *inactive* files and to destroy unnecessary papers. This transferring process is exceedingly important because it saves dollars and cents for any organization, large or small, in three ways. (1) It reduces the amount of office space needed for the active files. (2) It makes possible the use of inexpensive equipment and supplies for the inactive files. (3) It streamlines the active files, so that materials can be filed or located with the utmost efficiency.

Policy as to how long filed material is to be kept should be formulated in any organization after careful consideration has been given to the nature of the business, the type of papers handled, the information derived from them, and the law.

Such an analysis usually reveals the following four categories:

Vital papers. Essential to the existence of the business and irreplaceable if destroyed. They should never be transferred.

Important papers. They facilitate the routine of the business and are replaceable at great cost and much delay. They may be transferred if inactive and placed in cabinets that will keep them in good condition.

Useful papers. They are temporarily helpful and are replaceable at slight cost. They are often destroyed after three or four years.

Nonessential records. Material that can be destroyed after temporary use.

The following schedule for keeping records has been approved by the National Fire Protection Association. It may be adjusted to meet the requirements of almost any organization. The requirements set forth by Federal and state laws must be considered also.

Records That Must Be Kept Permanently

Capital stock and bond ledgers, and registers. In case of partnerships, all papers relating to the formation of the partnership.
Stockholders and directors minute books.
Deeds and other title papers and mortgages.
General ledgers, journals, and cashbooks.
Records of cost and inventory value of plant, equipment, and fixtures and supporting papers.
Records relating to insurance premiums and amounts recovered.
Copies of schedules and returns to authorities for tax purposes and records of appeal.
Audit reports.
Records and books relating to bills and notes payable.
Paid drafts, checks, and receipts for cash paid out.
Correspondence relating to stop-payment orders and issues of duplicate checks.

Payrolls, pay checks, and other evidences of payments for services.

Records That Must Be Kept Seven Years

List of holders of voting securities presented at meetings.
Records of interest coupons, paid and unpaid.
All contracts, leases, and agreements. (Retain seven years after expiration.)
Accounts receivable ledgers.
Schedules of fire and other insurance and papers substantiating claims.
Deposit books and record stubs.
Inventories of materials with record of adjustments.
Sales records.
Lists of summaries and of collections.
Records and reports of uncollectible accounts.

Records That Must Be Kept From Two to Three Years

Proxies of holders of voting securities.
Records and files of fidelity bonds of employees. (Retain three years after expiration.)

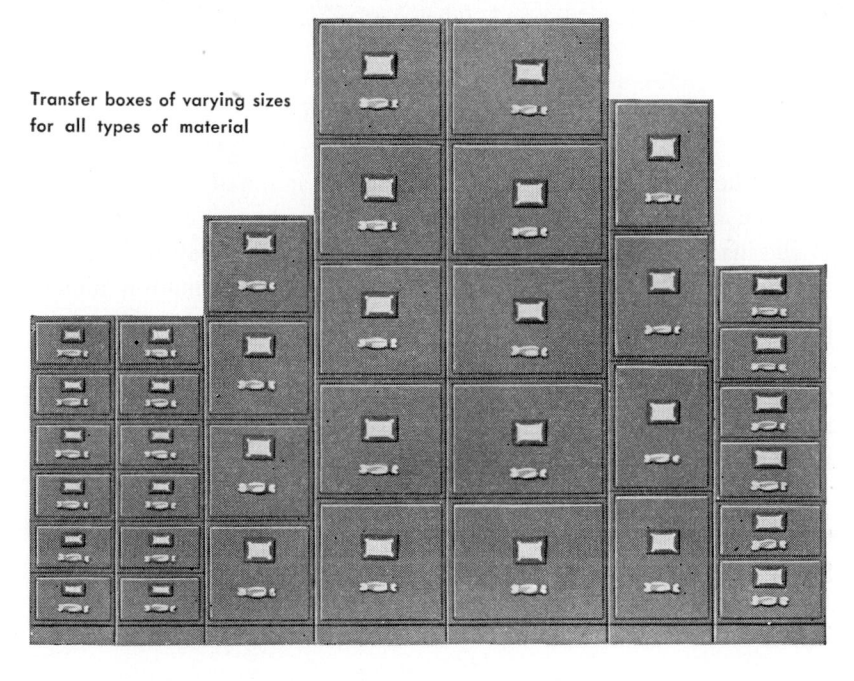

Transfer boxes of varying sizes for all types of material

Records of insurance policies in force and notices of changes in and cancellation of such policies. (Retain three years after expiration.)
Records relating to garnishments and assignments of employees' salaries.
Copies of purchase orders.
Ratings, credit classifications, and investigations of customers.
Liability and other insurance policies that have expired, but as to which unreported or pending claims might arise in the future.

Records That Must Be Kept One Year

Records and statements of deposits with banks; statements of interest due on daily balances and copies of bank deposit slips.

Plans of Transfer

There are several plans of transfer. The one selected should depend on the nature and frequency of reference, the space available, and the filing system in use. There are two general methods: periodic and perpetual. Each may be adapted to meet specific situations. To facilitate the finding of material, the arrangement of folders in the transfer equipment should correspond, whenever possible, to that used in the current files.

Periodic Transfer

Periodic transfer is the removal of papers at *stated intervals* (once or twice a year or at other definite times) from the current, active files to the inactive transfer equipment. Periodic transfer may be operated in one of three ways: one period, two period, or maximum-minimum period.

In the one-period plan, only the papers for the current filing period occupy the entire capacity of the active files. At stated intervals, *all* the folders and their contents of the current period are moved directly from the active files to the inactive; and a new filing period is started. The guides usually remain in the active files, and the transferred miscellaneous folders are placed in front of the alphabetic subdivision they govern to serve as guides in the inactive files. This eliminates the need for having a second set of expensive guides for the inactive files. New individual folders and miscellaneous folders are prepared for the active files. This transfer plan is a simple one, but it has a definite disadvantage. For a while, frequent trips will have to be made to the transfer files to consult still active material. If the transfer files are located outside the main office area, much valuable time will be lost.

In the two-period plan, the active files are divided to provide space for two classes of material—for current records and for papers from the last filing period. At the end of each filing period (three months, six months, a year or whatever length of time was selected between transfer times), all folders and their contents from the oldest filing period are moved to the transfer files. The two-period plan requires two sets of active guides and folders—one for the current and one for the last filing period—but it does eliminate the disadvantage of the one-period plan. Because only the older papers have been transferred, the current records and the material of the previous period are still readily available in the active files. The two illustrations below show how the file drawers may be arranged under a two-period plan to make the most accessible space available for the frequently used papers. Such arrangements will eliminate the fatigue that comes from working in a stooped or tip-toe position. The illustration on page 74 shows how

Two file arrangements for a two-period transfer plan, with easily accessible space for frequently used material

A-E ACTIVE	L-R ACTIVE
F-K ACTIVE	S-Z ACTIVE
A-E INACTIVE	L-R INACTIVE
F-K INACTIVE	S-Z INACTIVE

A-E INACTIVE	I-Q INACTIVE
A-B ACTIVE	M-N ACTIVE
C-F ACTIVE	O-S ACTIVE
G-L ACTIVE	T-Z ACTIVE
F-H INACTIVE	R-Z INACTIVE

the file drawers may be arranged under a two-period plan to halve the work at transfer time. Only the material in the inactive drawers needs to be emptied to ready them for current records. All that needs to be done to the other drawers, the ones that contain the current papers of the last filing period, is to change the identification cards in front, so that the material is labeled as inactive. *Double capacity*, *multiple transfer*, and *cycle method* are other terms sometimes used for the two-period plan.

In the maximum-minimum period plan, papers are moved directly from the active files to the transfer files. However, the disadvantage of the one-period plan is overcome by keeping some of the recent material in the current file. Under such a plan, the maximum and minimum periods must be established according to the needs of the organization. At the time of transfer, when the maximum period has been reached, all papers bearing a date prior to the minimum period are removed from the current file drawers to the transfer equipment. This plan requires the elimination of papers from each active folder between two fixed dates.

A-B ACTIVE	A-B INACTIVE	K-L ACTIVE	K-L INACTIVE
C ACTIVE	C INACTIVE	M-N ACTIVE	M-N INACTIVE
D-E ACTIVE	D-E INACTIVE	O-R ACTIVE	O-R INACTIVE
F-G ACTIVE	F-G INACTIVE	S ACTIVE	S INACTIVE
H-J ACTIVE	H-J INACTIVE	T-Z ACTIVE	T-Z INACTIVE

For example: suppose the nature of a business makes it wise for at least a year's correspondence to be kept in the current folders, and the volume of material filed makes transfer necessary every six months. Under the maximum-minimum plan, the minimum would be one year and the maximum 18 months. On January 1, 1955, therefore, there would be in the current files papers going back for a period of 18 months, or to July 1, 1953. The July, 1953, through December, 1953, papers would be removed, leaving on hand for reference papers of January, 1954, through December, 1954, or the material for one year. At transfer time six months later, or on June 1, 1955, there would again be an accumulation of 18 months' papers in the current files; and the material for the oldest six-month period—from January, 1954, through June, 1954—would be transferred. The material being transferred can be placed with previously transferred material, or it can be stored away in the transferred files by periods.

Perpetual Transfer

Under the perpetual plan, papers are being transferred from the current to inactive files all the time. It is generally used when the nature of the business makes it difficult to set definite periods for transfer. In the type of work done by contractors, architects, or lawyers, the length of time taken to complete the work varies with each job or case. Transferring files on a set-time basis might result, therefore, in the removal of active material. Whenever a specific job or case is completed, all papers pertaining to it are moved to the inactive files.

Planning Transfer

Doing the following things before the time of actual transfer will lighten the file worker's burden at transfer time. Interference with regular use of the files will also be reduced.

1. Plan the new active files by preparing a list of those correspondents or subjects that will need new folders. Eliminating individual folders for those whose activity is no longer sufficient will save filing space.
2. Type up the labels for the new folders. Many organizations have found that using different-colored labels for each filing period re-

duces the possibility of confusing active and inactive materials.
3. Make sure transfer files or boxes are available. Affix labels to them that will show clearly what the contents will be and for what period of time.
4. Papers no longer necessary should be removed from the transfer files and destroyed. No papers should be destroyed without authority, preferably in writing.

Microfilming

Microfilming, or microphotography as it is sometimes known, is a relatively new technique of filing business records. It is a means of photographing papers in a greatly reduced size, maintaining the film either in rolls or strips. When required, the images can be viewed on some form of projector that usually shows them enlarged at approximately the original size of the documents.

Almost all transferred records lend themselves perfectly to storage on microfilm. But microfilming is not restricted to transferred or stored records. Many current operations, involving large quantities of inactive or semiactive records, are recorded on microfilm to save space. Banks use microfilming for obtaining copies of canceled checks; department stores, dairies, and bus companies, for billing operations; railroads, for freight waybill handling; and publications, for subscription work. In other words, microphotography is an aid, not only in the filing department, but in other operations of business as well.

It is estimated that microfilming will save approximately 98 per cent of the space normally used to house the full-size original papers. Most business papers are photographed on 16mm film on reels holding 100 feet of film and maintained in boxes 4- by 4- by 1-inch. A 100-foot roll of film will hold 13,000 bank checks, or 5,800 4- by 6-inch cards, or 3,000 letters. Since the average well-guided letter-size file drawer holds about 3,000 documents, exclusive of guides or folders, the resulting saving in space is apparent. Another concept of the spacesaving possibilities can be obtained when it is realized that one microfilm file cabinet like the one illustrated will hold on rolls of film the contents of at least 160 four-drawer letter-size files.

The spacesaving advantage of microfilming cuts costs by reducing the space needed for files, by reducing the number of files required,

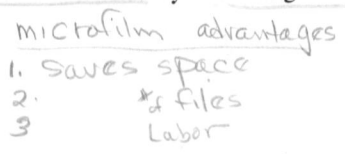

TRANSFER METHODS | 77

The open box on top of the microfilm filing cabinet contained a roll of film which has been placed in the reading machine at the right.

and by reducing the labor needed to procure filed records. In addition to the spacesaving advantage of microphotography, many organizations are using it to make copies of their important records, which can be stored in a small space away from the original location to protect them against fire, loss, theft, and bombings.

The papers to be microfilmed can be arranged in alphabetic order or in any other order according to any of the standard methods of filing before being put through the photographing machine. In that way the film will be self-indexing. The photographing machine may

78 | PROGRESSIVE FILING

also be equipped with certain devices that can be changed as required. These devices will appear at the proper places on the film and will perform the function of the guide notations in a file drawer.

The outside of the box, in which the reel of film is kept, will indicate what is on the reel; and the film file drawer, which contains many of these boxes, will also have labels to help locate desired information.

The photographing machines come in two types, one that requires manual feeding of papers into the machine and the other that does it automatically. Papers can be fed manually into the machines at the rate of 60 to 80 a minute depending on the type of document. The machines have automatic safeguards that indicate when two papers have been fed in simultaneously or when a paper has been fed in improperly, so that a proper picture cannot be obtained.

These men are feeding records into the photographing machine.

The film-reading machines, which are actually a type of motion-picture projector, can be operated either manually or electrically. These reading machines show the documents in their original size or larger for easy reading.

The *microcard* is also an application of microphotography. When microcards are used, the original documents are not reduced as much in size when they are photographed. Thus all information is easily read with average eyesight, eliminating the need for the film-reading machines. Obviously, microcards will not save as much space as microfilms. Film strips are attached to microcards

QUESTIONS

for Review and Discussion

1. What factors are considered in deciding what records to keep and where to keep them?
2. Why must the amount of office space devoted to filing be limited?
3. For what are active and inactive files used?
4. What does the term "transferring" mean in filing?
5. How does transferring reduce the cost of filing?
6. What determines how long an organization will keep filed material?
7. When analyzing filed material for transfer, what are the four categories of importance?
8. What is the difference between periodic and perpetual transfer?
9. Explain the one-period plan of periodic transfer.
10. What is the principal disadvantage of the one-period plan?
11. Explain the two-period plan of periodic transfer.
12. What are other names for the two-period transfer plan?
13. How can the proper arrangement of file drawers in the two-period plan help reduce fatigue?
14. Explain the maximum-minimum plan of periodic transfer.
15. Under what conditions is it wise to use the perpetual transfer method?
16. What activities can be performed in advance to facilitate transfer?
17. What is microfilming?
18. Make several comparisons of the space requirements of filing full-size original papers and filing by microphotography.
19. How does microfilming cut filing costs?
20. Name another use being made of microfilming in addition to the space-saving advantage.
21. How is a specific item of microfilmed material located?
22. What two kinds of machines are needed in the microfilming process?

Chapter 7

Selection of Equipment and Supplies

Need for Proper Selection

You've made a good start on the road toward filing efficiency if you have selected a filing system that is tailored to the needs of your organization. Applying basic rules of filing and using proper techniques of charge-out, follow-up, and transfer will avoid detours and keep you on the right road. But to get to your objective with more speed and less fatigue, you must be sure to have the equipment and supplies that will enable your system and methods to function at their best. Don't get the idea that all filing equipment is pretty much alike, and that it doesn't make much difference what you buy. There is an unbelievable variety in the filing supplies available to modern business. And if you can't find what you would like in size, shape, material, or price range in the ready-made merchandise, you can have it custom made. Visit

80

the business shows and keep your eyes on the show windows of your local stationers and business-equipment dealers. But no matter how you do it, make sure you keep in touch with the latest developments in filing. It will not only make you more efficient at your work, but it will also make that work easier.

Cabinets

Don't practice false economy when you purchase your cabinets. They are obtainable in many grades. Business has found, however, that the best-quality equipment is the most economical, because it lasts longer and gives more satisfactory service. Remember that a letter-size file drawer usually carries a load of 60 to 70 pounds. Make sure, therefore, that the drawers have telescoping slides that will give support when they are fully extended. In addition, the drawers should operate on ball-bearing rollers, so that they can be opened and closed with a minimum of effort. The frame of the cabinet should be adequately reinforced to give strength and rigidity.

Steel cabinets seem to be replacing the wooden ones slowly but surely. Both are available in a variety of finishes, and you will have little difficulty in making a selection that will fit into the color scheme of your office.

Because the drawers are not always filled to capacity, there should be some provision, other than just the back of the drawer, for keeping the filed material in an upright position. Usually movable blocks are used for this purpose. These compressors, or *followers* as they are sometimes called, should slide easily and yet should hold the material securely in the desired position. They must not be too bulky, or they will occupy valuable filing space. The file drawer should also provide for some means of holding the guides in place, so that they will not "ride up" or be lifted out accidentally when folders are withdrawn.

Papers will become dog-eared, folders and guides will be short-lived, and the drawers will be slovenly in appearance, if filed material is either too tight or too loose. Filing cabinets, however, are obtainable that automatically give you a V-shaped work space for easier removal and insertion of papers and folders. One model has a drop front that eases the tension on the filed material when the drawer is open and

FlexiFile with cloth pockets

Super-Filer with drop front and self-adjusting dividers

Courtesy General Fireproofing Co.

V-CUT POCKET

TRI-GUARD SUPPORT

V-cut pocket

Courtesy Globe-Wernicke Co.

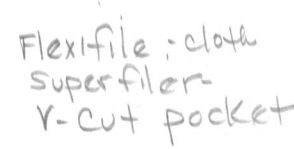

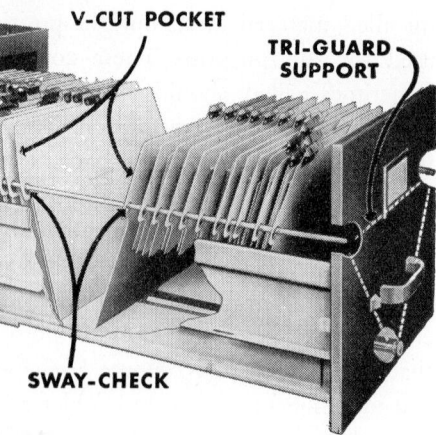

SWAY-CHECK

82

A blueprint file

A cabinet for special records

83

84 | PROGRESSIVE FILING

tightens up the material when the drawer is closed. Another model gives you the same result by a drawer back that expands when the drawer is opened.

You can get file drawers that will accommodate 5-by-3 cards, 6-by-4 cards, checks, tabulating-machine cards, letters, legal documents, blueprints; in fact, there is a size to store just about any standard-size record you can think of.

For additional flexibility, there are drawer dividers that will enable you to partition off your filing space any way you want. To further meet your needs, you can have cabinets in about any size and arrangement you want: one or two drawers high for next to desks; three drawers high to form counters; four or five drawers high for ordinary purposes; and in batteries to form work alcoves or partitions.

This arrangement of cabinets—housing cards, correspondence folders, and records—also serves as a counter.

EQUIPMENT AND SUPPLIES | **85**

Transfer cabinets are exposed to relatively little wear and tear, because the inactive papers stored in them are seldom referred to. Inexpensive equipment can, therefore, be used safely. This is available in corrugated fiberboard, in metal, or in a combination of both. Some cabinets are drawer style, and others open from the top like ordinary boxes.

Visible filing equipment also comes in a large assortment of sizes and types. There are rotary wheels, shelf trays, rotary trays, vertical compartments, and books. Some provide for protection of the record by a covering of transparent material. The papers are fastened to the equipment in various ways. What type you select should be determined by the amount of material to be housed and whether or not that material is to be used for reference or recording purposes. More than likely, one type will enable you to do your work faster and with less effort than another. So be sure to look all of them over carefully before you make your selection.

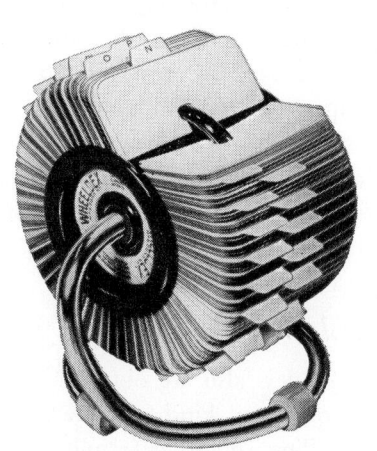

A rotary visible card index

Courtesy Wheeldex Mfg. Co., Inc.
A rotary wheel card file

Guides

The number of guides used and their position depends on the filing system being used. The purpose of guides, however, is the same in all systems—to guide the eye in finding and filing papers and to support the folders. Guides are available in all standard drawer sizes as well as for special systems, such as fingerprint, hospital, and insurance files. Guides made of Manila stock are inexpensive and will serve in transfer files or other places where there is little activity; but, where traffic is heavy, guides made of heavy Bristol or pressboard should be used. They are strong enough to be durable and rigid enough to serve in their supporting function. Guides are manufactured with the tab or upper-edge projection in various positions, so that they may be used in any type of filing system. In some cases, the tab is the same material as the guide, with the caption printed or with a place for a label; in others, there is a place to insert the caption either with or without a transparent covering. The insert tabs are made of a variety of materials and are attached to the guide in many different ways. Make sure they are fastened correctly, so that they will not scratch your hands or that papers will not catch on them. You can get tabs slanted for easier vision and even tabs that magnify the guide caption. Remember, the guides are the signposts of your filing system; it is worth spending some extra money for speedier, more accurate reading and for longer-lasting materials.

Folders

Folders also are obtainable in a variety of styles and materials. The amount and kind of material to be filed, and the type and extent of handling should determine your selection. For ordinary use, Manila and kraft folders come in different weights. You can have them with straight edges or with tabs in various positions. Some are reinforced along the top where the greatest wear occurs. Folders can be obtained that are triple scored on the bottom to allow for expansion. As the number of papers increases, a new fold is made along one of the scored lines to widen the bottom. This permits all papers to drop to the bottom and distributes the weight evenly.

Folders
1. Top-straight edge
2. Celluloid angle tab
3. ½ cut right-end tab
4. Metal fastener inside folder
5. Reinforced individual tab
6. Celluloid tab for removable label
7. Armor-clad metal tip tab
8. ⅕ cut plain tab
9. Straight-edge leatherette expansion folder
10. Leatherette envelope with tape

87

88 | PROGRESSIVE FILING

There are a number of folders for special needs. Envelope folders are practical when the volume of papers is large or when material is carried around considerably. For follow-up work, folders with adjustable signals, by their position, remind you of a special date. Hanging folders, which are suspended on a metal frame placed inside the regular file drawer, keep the papers neat and straight, allow for expansion, and eliminate the need for the compressor block. Under certain conditions, it may be advantageous to use folders that are folded at the end rather than on the bottom; or when papers are accumulated without a folder, you can get file backs that are strong sheets of Manila used to back up the papers that are to be fastened.

A filing stool eliminates stooping when working at low drawers.

This FlexiFile, consisting of heavy cloth pockets, allows for easy expansion by eliminating compressor blocks.

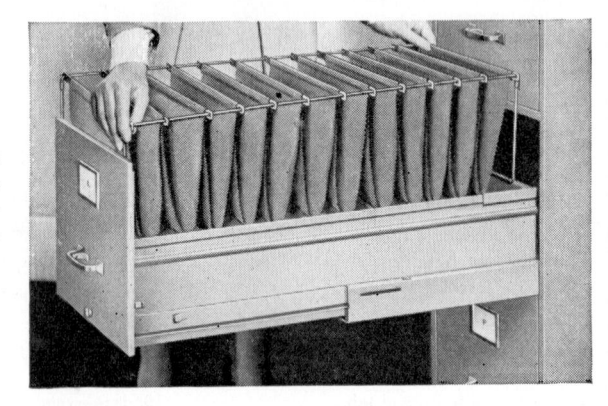

Miscellaneous Filing Aids

Labels to identify the drawers, guides, and folders are available in many styles. They are obtainable printed or blank, gummed or plain. Different colors are obtainable for classification purposes. As an aid in preparing them, they even come rolled in a special package that you can rest on the typewriter roller. All you have to do is tear off the label along the perforated lines.

In addition to the colored labels for classification purposes, there are colored signals that can be placed in various positions to guide your eye to pertinent information. They can be obtained in fixed or movable types, made of paper, plastic, or metal compositions.

When there is considerable need for securing material together, various sorts of fasteners group the papers compactly and eliminate the one-sided bulkiness and catching that paper clips, staples, or ordinary fasteners create.

Whenever printed forms are needed, whether they be standard ones like cross-reference sheets or unusual ones for special situations, they can be obtained or specially designed by the filing-equipment companies.

Innumerable accessories are available to lighten filing tasks—stools to reduce the stop-and-squat fatigue of filing in lower drawers; movable shelves that can be hooked on to the drawer handle to provide work space within easy reach; sorter equipment of all types to speed up the preliminary arranging of material before the actual filing; and many kinds of trays and stands.

Remember that the filing-equipment companies have the knowledge, equipment, and desire to help you. Don't be bashful about asking them for advice, even if you are not in the immediate market to purchase anything. Have at least one filing catalogue handy on your office reference shelf, so that you can consult it for filing ideas.

Moveable signals are illustrated on page 141; fasteners, on page 87; a cross-reference sheet, on page 35; a hanging file shelf, on page 37; sorters, on pages 34 and 38.

QUESTIONS

for Review and Discussion

1. Why are the best-quality file cabinets usually the most economical?
2. What feature will make it easier to open a file drawer?
3. What is the purpose of a file-drawer follower, and what characteristics should it have?
4. What types of file cabinets are available to give work space without loss of filing space?
5. What are drawer dividers?
6. Name some possible arrangements of file cabinets and the purpose of each.
7. How do transfer cabinets differ from regular file cabinets?
8. Name some forms of visible equipment.
9. In what materials are guides available, and what determines the one to be used?
10. Describe some of the guide tabs available.
11. What is the purpose of scoring a folder?
12. What is an envelope folder?
13. Describe the function of a follow-up folder.
14. What are the advantages of a "hanging" folder?
15. What is a "file back"?
16. Enumerate the different types of filing labels available.
17. What are "signals"?
18. What is the advantage of using a filing stool? a filing shelf?
19. Describe the types of sorting equipment available.

Chapter 8

Numeric Correspondence Filing

Nature of Numeric Filing

In alphabetic systems, names are used for guide and folder captions. *Numeric* filing systems are so called because numbers are used as code captions on the guide and folder tabs. Alphabetic systems are direct systems because a person can go directly to the file drawer and, by means of the name captions, file or find materials. Numeric systems are indirect because in most cases, before papers can be placed in or taken from the file drawer, the worker must refer to an alphabetic card index to ascertain the number assigned to a specific name or subject.

Despite the indirectness, numeric filing systems can be used to advantage under the following circumstances:

1. In businesses where papers would group themselves around definite cases, contracts, or operations that are active for reasonably long

Illustration courtesy Mutual Life Insurance Co.

but indefinite periods and that require permanent and extensive cross reference. For example, a lawyer may represent the same client in a number of cases. By having a separate numbered folder for each case, he can locate papers faster than by mixing all the papers of the different cases in one folder bearing the client's name. Similar conditions exist in offices of architects, contractors, and engineers.

2. In business operations where the term of reference is a number rather than a name. Some departments within a business are concerned with a phase of activity that does not relate primarily to a person's name. It is, therefore, sometimes more efficient to organize department records around numbers. For example, accounting departments quite often file vouchers by their numbers; manufacturing departments and storerooms refer to, and frequently file, orders by the order number rather than by the name of the customer; insurance companies usually use policy numbers rather than the policyholder's name. In confidential situations, names can be concealed from those handling the files by the use of number captions.

Organization of a Numeric Correspondence File

There are three parts in most numeric systems of filing:

1. The main correspondence file for *active* correspondents or subjects in which the guides and folders bear numeric captions.
2. A miscellaneous correspondence file for inactive correspondents or subjects in which the guides and folders bear alphabetic captions.
3. A card index in which the names of correspondents or subjects are arranged alphabetically. When papers are to be filed or found, this index is consulted to ascertain the numeric caption of the folder.

Main Numeric File

In numeric filing, a number is assigned consecutively to each *active* correspondent and subject as it develops. A number once assigned is maintained until a correspondent no longer does business with the firm or a subject ceases to exist. After a specified period, the number may be reassigned. All papers pertaining to the correspondent or subject are placed in a folder bearing the number assigned to that correspondent or subject.

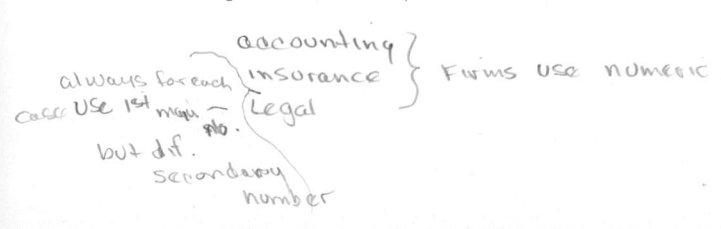

A numeric file

An index to the above numeric file, showing the number 946 assigned to Electric Production Station Supplies

93

As with alphabetic systems, different methods of arranging the guides are in use. In the method illustrated, the guides are in five positions, staggered across the file drawer from left to right. The captions can be numbered in 10's or 20's.

All folders in the main numeric file are individual folders. They are arranged in numerical sequence in back of the proper guide. Usually straight-edge folders, that is, folders with no tabs, are used. Generally the numbers are printed on the back flap of the folder in the upper right-hand corner, although some file workers like to have the number printed on the front flap as well. As in alphabetic individual folders, the arrangement of papers within the folders is according to date with the latest date in front or on top.

When a folder reaches its capacity, it can be subdivided by date or subject, according to the way the papers will be requested. Subdivided folders generally bear auxiliary numbers to help identify them. For example, folder 206 upon being subdivided would become 206-1 and the new folder would be 206-2. Both would be arranged in sequence behind folder 205.

In other plans for arranging guides and folders in a numeric system, the guides appear in two or three positions at the left only; and folders with tabs are used generally in the last position on the right.

Miscellaneous Alphabetic File

A number and a place in the main numeric file are not assigned to a correspondent or subject until sufficient material has accumulated. Until then, such inactive items are filed alphabetically in the miscellaneous file. This miscellaneous alphabetic file can be kept in the front part of the first filing drawer of the main numeric file, in a separate drawer of the main numeric file, or in an entirely separate filing cabinet.

When enough papers, usually five pieces, have accumulated under one name or subject in the miscellaneous file, the first unused number is assigned to that name or subject; and the papers are placed in the folder of that number and removed to the main numeric file.

Unused supplies are kept in a convenient place, usually in an empty file drawer. The file number for a new name is determined by checking the first unused folder; sometimes a register is kept showing the names and numbers assigned.

Card Index

A numeric system cannot be operated without a card index that will identify the assigned numbers. Each card contains the name of a correspondent or subject and the number of the folder that has been assigned. The symbol *M* is used on the cards of inactive correspondents or subjects to indicate that such materials are being filed in the miscellaneous alphabetic file. This *M* is replaced by a permanent number if the correspondent or subject becomes active enough to warrant a separate folder in the main numeric correspondence file. All cards in the index are arranged alphabetically.

Cross Reference

In alphabetic systems, a cross-reference sheet telling where the document is actually filed is placed in all other folders where a person might look. In numeric systems, cross-referencing is done only in the card index. As the illustration shows, a person seeking information in the card index about the Carter Bread Company would be referred to the Homemade Bakeries in folder number 248.

Numeric Filing Procedure

The steps in numeric filing to be performed are quite similar to those followed in alphabetic filing.

A cross reference in the index to the numeric file

```
Carter Bread Company
Chicago, Illinois


See:  Homemade Bakeries                         248
```

Inspecting. Each piece of correspondence is checked to make sure it has been released for filing.

Alphabetic indexing and coding. The name or subject under which the paper is to be filed is determined and underlined. Names for cross-referencing should be selected and indicated also.

Alphabetic sorting. The papers are arranged alphabetically according to the coded names to expedite the use of the card index.

Numeric coding. The file number, ascertained from the card index, is placed in the upper right-hand corner of each paper. If the card index shows that no number has been assigned to a correspondent or subject, an *M* is placed in the upper right-hand corner to indicate that the paper is to be filed in the miscellaneous alphabetic file. A colored pencil is preferred for coding purposes.

Numeric sorting. The papers are arranged first by hundreds, then by tens, and then finally into correct numeric sequence. The papers coded *M* are all placed in one pile during the numeric sorting and are then arranged separately according to the alphabetic sorting technique suggested.

Filing. All materials coded *M* are placed in the proper folder in the miscellaneous alphabetic file. The papers bearing code numbers are placed in the folders bearing those numbers in the main numeric file. Care must be exercised in reading the coded numbers and the folder numbers to avoid transposition of figures. Number 1324 is very easily read as 1342. Yet such an error is not as likely to be noticed as a misspelled name. Because such errors are so easily made and so difficult to locate, many organizations with numeric filing systems make provision for checking them periodically.

Other Numeric Filing Methods

The consecutive-number or serial-number type of numeric filing just discussed is the most commonly used of the numeric systems. There are two other kinds: significant-number systems and terminal-digit systems. As the names imply, the numbers do not just run in sequence as in the consecutive type of numeric filing; instead, the numbers are assigned to classify and group. Such systems can be learned readily in the specific situations where they are used, if the basic principles of consecutive numeric filing are understood.

QUESTIONS

for Review and Discussion

1. What is numeric filing?
2. What is meant by direct or indirect filing systems?
3. Where can numeric filing systems be used to advantage?
4. What are the three parts of a numeric system?
5. How long is an assigned number kept by a correspondent or subject?
6. Are there any miscellaneous folders in the main numeric file?
7. Where is a number printed on a folder?
8. What is the arrangement of papers within a numbered folder?
9. What is done when a numbered folder reaches its capacity?
10. How are guides and folders arranged in a numeric system?
11. Why is a card index needed in numeric filing?
12. What does the symbol M on a card in the card index mean?
13. How are cards arranged in a card index?
14. Why is a miscellaneous alphabetic file needed in a numeric system?
15. Where is the miscellaneous alphabetic part of a numeric system kept?
16. When is a correspondent or subject assigned a number in a numeric system? What number is assigned?
17. Compare cross-referencing in alphabetic and numeric systems.
18. Enumerate and describe the steps in numeric filing procedure.
19. What is a common cause of error in numeric filing? What safeguard can be adopted?
20. What are some numeric filing systems other than the consecutive-number type?

Chapter 9

Geographic Correspondence Filing

Nature of Geographic Filing

Geographic filing is an alphabetic arrangement of papers first by location and then by name or subject. It has advantages for businesses that conduct, analyze, and control their operations on a geographic district basis. Sales organizations find a geographic arrangement helpful for keeping track of salesmen and customers within an area. Businesses that have branch offices must differentiate among the activities of the different branches and frequently do it on a geographic basis. The United States Post Offices do not accept second-class mail unless it is separated by state and town; therefore, companies that send out large quantities of mail second-class, usually organize their mailing lists and files geographically. Public utilities, real estate firms, and government offices, from the nature of their activities, often find it advantageous to organize their files on a geographic basis.

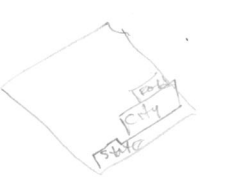

GEOGRAPHIC CORRESPONDENCE FILING | 99

How a business organizes a geographic filing system will depend on the type of business, the use made of the filed material, and the geographic locations in which the company has activity. However, although there may be and should be differences within geographic systems to fit the needs of specific businesses, certain basic fundamentals are common to all geographic filing systems.

Arrangement of the File Drawer

The primary guides generally bear the names of the largest or most important geographic divisions occurring in the operations of the business. The secondary guides are used for subdivisions of the main geographic units, as well as for alphabetic sections of the geographic divisions and subdivisions.

In the geographic file illustrated on page 100, the arrangement of the guide and folder tabs from left to right is: (1) state and alphabetic guides, (2) town or city guides or alphabetic subdivisions of those towns or cities, (3) miscellaneous folders, (4) individual folders, (5) special guides. The arrangement of the guides and folders from the front to the back of the file drawer is: (1) state guide, (2) alphabetic guide, (3) town or city guide, (4) individual folders arranged alphabetically by correspondent, (5) miscellaneous folders for town or city, (6) miscellaneous state folders.

In the file illustrated, the largest geographic divisions are the states; and the subdivisions are cities or towns. Some businesses, however, might use foreign countries as the main unit and towns or cities as the subdivisions; others might use towns or cities as the main unit and streets as the subdivision. The geographic district used will be determined by the filing needs of the business.

Folders

Individual folders are made out whenever a correspondent is active enough to justify one. The folder captions list the name of the city or town first, the name of the state second, and then the name of the correspondent. The reason for listing the city or town name first is that the city or town guide is nearer in the drawer than the state guide,

100 | PROGRESSIVE FILING

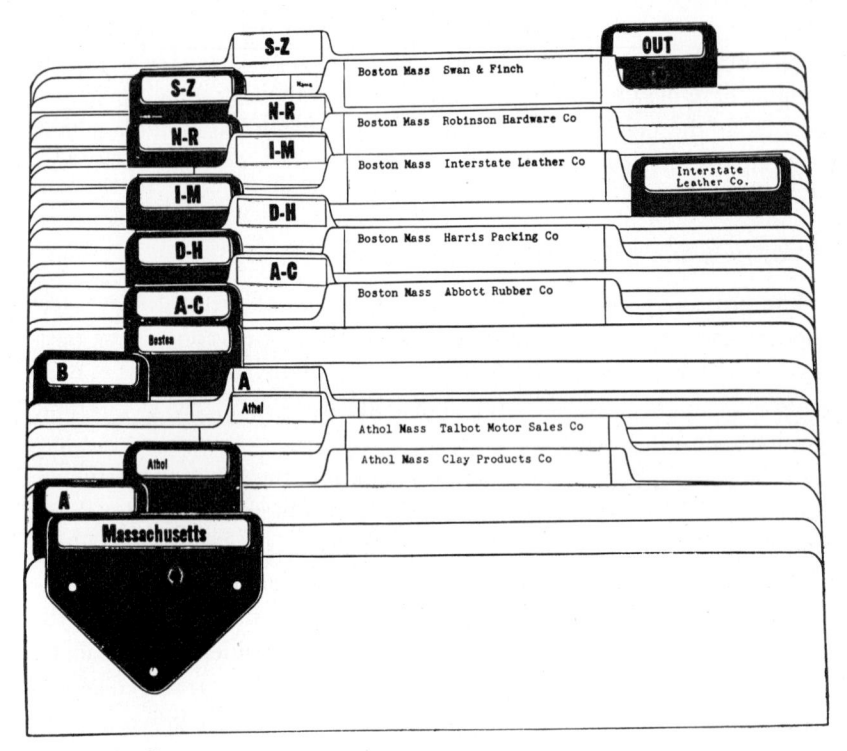

A geographic file

thereby making it easier to check for correct filing. Correspondence within the individual folders is arranged according to date, the latest date to the front or on top.

There are two kinds of miscellaneous folders—town or city miscellaneous folders and state miscellaneous folders. The papers of an inactive correspondent are filed in the state miscellaneous folder until enough papers have accumulated pertaining to one town or city to justify opening a miscellaneous folder for that town or city. Papers in the town or city miscellaneous folders are arranged alphabetically by name of correspondent. Papers in the state miscellaneous folders are arranged first alphabetically by the name of the town or city and then alphabetically by the name of the correspondent.

Card Index

A card index is not so necessary in a geographic file as it is in the numeric system. It is helpful, however, when a person requesting material from the files does not recall the geographic location involved. Each card contains the name of a correspondent and the geographic location. The cards are arranged alphabetically by names of correspondents.

Cross Reference

When cross reference is necessary from one location to another, it is done by means of a cross-reference sheet, if the cross reference occurs in a single letter only and is not likely to occur again. If it is a permanent cross reference from one location to another, the Manila tabbed cross-reference form is used. For example, the General Electric Company of Schenectady, New York, has many subsidiary offices, located in different parts of the country, one of which is the Holophane Works of Cleveland, Ohio. In order to keep all this company correspondence together, it is indexed and filed under Schenectady, New York, and a Manila tabbed cross-reference form is made out, since this is a permanent cross reference, as:

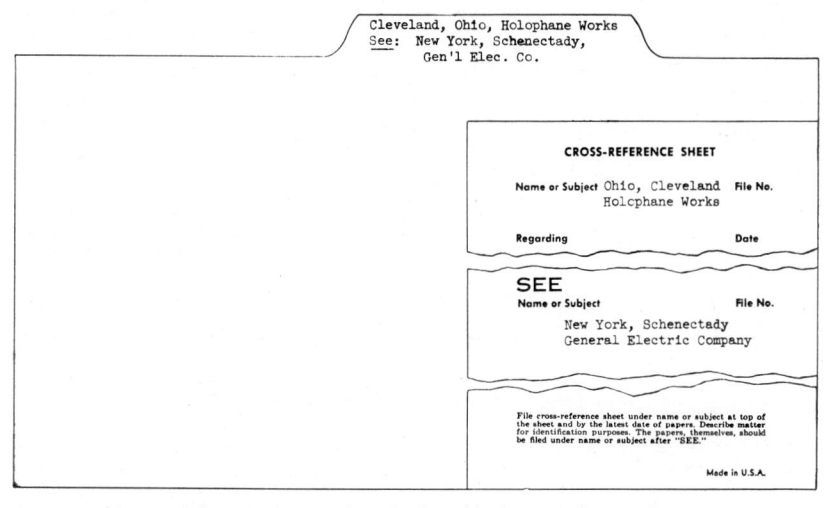

```
Cleveland, Ohio, Holophane Works
See:   New York, Schenectady,
       Gen'l Elec. Co.
```

CROSS-REFERENCE SHEET

Name or Subject Ohio, Cleveland File No.
                 Holophane Works

Regarding   Date

SEE
Name or Subject   File No.
       New York, Schenectady
       General Electric Company

File cross-reference sheet under name or subject at top of the sheet and by the latest date of papers. Describe matter for identification purposes. The papers, themselves, should be filed under name or subject after "SEE."

Made in U.S.A.

A geographic cross-reference sheet and a Manila tabbed cross-reference form

Cross reference from an individual to a location is possible only when a card index is maintained. For example, all correspondence in connection with the Caulon Press of New York is done directly with Mr. P. S. Henderson. Although the correspondence is indexed and filed geographically under New York, New York, Caulon Press, it might also be called for under Mr. Henderson's name. A card made out under the name of Henderson, P. S., referring to New York, New York, Caulon Press, is filed alphabetically in the card index.

Geographic Filing Procedure

The steps to be performed are quite similar to those followed in alphabetic filing:

Inspecting. Each piece of correspondence is checked to make sure it has been released for filing.

Indexing and coding. The name of the correspondent and location under which the paper is to be filed are determined and marked. Names for cross-referencing should be selected and indicated also. Some file workers like to differentiate between the coding of a correspondent's name and the geographic location by underlining one and encircling the other.

Sorting. Papers are sorted first by main geographic divisions. Then these main units are sorted into the geographic subdivisions. Where there is a large volume in any subdivision, it is further sorted by alphabetic sections.

Filing. The state and city or town guides are used to locate the proper folder section rapidly. The appropriate alphabetic part of the folder section is then scanned for an individual folder for the coded name. If there is none, the paper is placed in a miscellaneous folder.

QUESTIONS

for Review and Discussion

1. What is a geographic file?
2. Name some businesses that use geographic filing.
3. What determines how a business organizes its geographic file?

GEOGRAPHIC CORRESPONDENCE FILING | 103

4. Describe one possible arrangement of guides and folders from left to right in a geographic file drawer; from front to back.
5. Name some divisions and subdivisions that could be used for primary and secondary guide captions in a geographic file drawer.
6. In a geographic file, when are individual folders made out?
7. In what order is information listed in the caption of a geographic individual folder?
8. How is correspondence arranged within a geographic individual folder?
9. What are the two types of miscellaneous folders in a geographic file, and for what are they used?
10. How is correspondence arranged in each type of miscellaneous folder?
11. For what purpose is a card index used in a geographic file?
12. How can cross-referencing be done in a geographic file?
13. Enumerate and describe the steps in the geographic filing procedure.

Chapter 10

Subject Correspondence Filing

Nature of Subject Filing

In *subject filing,* material is arranged by names of topics or things, rather than by names of people, companies, or location. Subject files, or data or topical files as they are also referred to, are used for the main files of a business when material is of a technical or statistical nature, because the grouping of such papers brings out relationships not apparent under other systems. Subject files are often used for storing the records of specific divisions or departments or individuals within an organization. Because management concerns itself more with the complete picture rather than with isolated details, the private files of executives quite often must provide for subject arrangement. The sales manager would be more likely to need information about milk sales, cheese sales, ice-cream sales, returned sales, flavors, sales predictions, etc., than about Fred Lacey or any other customer. The sales manager's files, therefore, could be on a subject basis, whereas the credit department or billing department or other department interested in specific individuals would maintain their files on an alphabetic or geographic basis.

Because subject filing actually is filing by description and different people do not always describe the same thing in the same manner, subject filing is not so easy to use as the alphabetic, geographic, or numeric methods where specific names or numbers are used as the guide or folder captions. The name *Brown* would not be confused with *Johnson* in an alphabetic file, or *Baltimore* with *Detroit* in a geographic file, or *1289* with *3621* in a numeric file; but in a subject file, material filed under the caption *Typewriter* might be requested under the heading of *Writing Machines* or *Office Machines*.

Kinds of Subject Files

When the volume of correspondence to be grouped by subject is small compared with matter to be filed by name, both subject matter and name matter may be filed in the same files using an alphabetic or any other name-filing system. A folder would simply be made out bearing a subject caption instead of a name caption. For instance, a folder for *Advertising* may be filed after a folder for *Adams Company* and before a folder for *Aero Club*.

Where the bulk of the material to be filed is by subject and those subjects may be grouped into main headings and then subdivided into specific classifications, a separate subject file is advisable.

Two systems may be used for filing papers by subject, and two arrangements are possible under each of these systems:

Alphabetic arrangements are:

Dictionary—where there is no logical connection between the subjects filed behind each other except the alphabetic sequence, as with the following folder captions: stationery, tanks, tape, tires.

Encyclopedic—where the subjects are grouped by logical relationships as well as in alphabetic sequence, as with the following folder captions after the main heading of tires: airplane, automobile, bicycle, motorcycle.

Numeric arrangements are:

Decimal—where subjects are grouped logically according to the

Dewey Decimal System used in public libraries and other specialized businesses.

Duplex-numeric—where subjects are grouped logically, with the main headings numbered in sequence and divisions or subdivisions designated by auxiliary numbers, letters, or both.

Choice of Subject Headings

Two things are necessary in any subject file, regardless of the system to be used: a subject classification and a relative index, which is really a cross reference of the subject classification.

The subject classification is a list of the main headings, divisions, and subdivisions and is arranged according to the system of filing to be used. If the alphabetic system is used, the main headings are arranged in exact alphabetic order; the divisions are arranged alphabetically under the main headings; and the subdivisions, alphabetically under the divisions. If the numeric system is used, the main headings are arranged in numeric order; the divisions, in numeric order under the main headings; and the subdivisions, in numeric order under the divisions.

The relative index is an alphabetic arrangement of all main headings, divisions, and subdivisions, irrespective of the main headings under which they may be grouped. Thus if a main heading is known but not a division or subdivision, the subject classification can be referred to. If a division or subdivision is known but not the main heading, the relative index would tell which main heading is to be used. Compare the order of topics in the partial subject classification and relative index that follow.

Subject Classification	*Relative Index*
Advertising	Advertising
Contracts	Applications
Prospects	Contracts—advertising
Applications	Correspondents—applications
Correspondents	Office Assistants—applications
Office Assistants	Prospects—advertising

The subject headings to be used should be selected by a person who knows the activities of the business well. The main headings should be simple, logical, comprehensive, and as few as possible. If possible, a single word, preferably a plural noun that best describes the topic, should be selected. When the main heading is extensive, it may be divided and then subdivided by function, item, person, place, or time. The divisions must be kept consistent, however. Dividing the main heading *Furniture* into *modern, maple,* and *living-room* would be incorrect, because one subdivision describes the type of material; another, the place of use; and the other, the style. Dividing *Furniture* into *living-room, dining-room, bedroom,* and *miscellaneous* and then subdividing each of these into *walnut, maple, mahogany* would be a consistent classification that would expedite filing and finding.

Because subject files must meet the needs of the individual business, it is unlikely that two subject classifications will ever be exactly alike. The following, however, is a partial list of printed classifications that can be referred to and adapted to a firm's needs.

Accounting, American Institute of Accountants, New York.
Agricultural Index, H. W. Wilson, New York.
Architecture, University of Illinois, Urbana.
Current List of Medical Literature, Army Medical Library, Washington, D. C.
Electricity, General Electric Catalog, Schenectady, New York.
Engineering Index, University of Illinois, Urbana.
Harvard Classification for Business Literature, H. W. Wilson, New York.
Library of Congress List of Subject Headings, Washington, D. C.
List of Subject Headings, American Library Association, Chicago.
Subject Headings for Financial Libraries, Special Libraries Association, New York.

Arrangement of the File Drawer—Subject Alphabetic

Many acceptable arrangements of guides and folders are available for a subject alphabetic file. The one illustrated on page 108 is distributed by Remington Rand. The main-division and subdivision guide captions are printed or typed on removable inserts.

Arrangement of the File Drawer—Subject Numeric

When a permanent grouping together of related material becomes necessary with minute divisions and subdivisions of each group or sub-

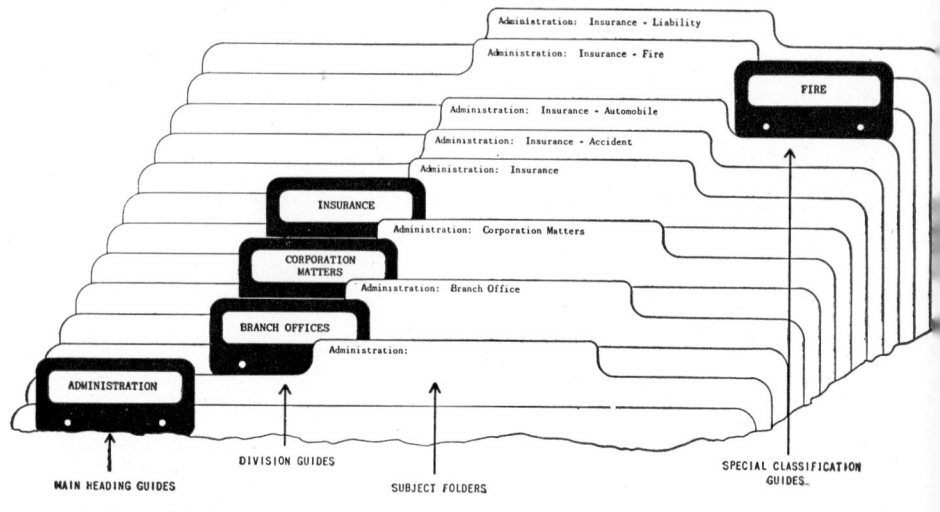

A subject alphabetic file

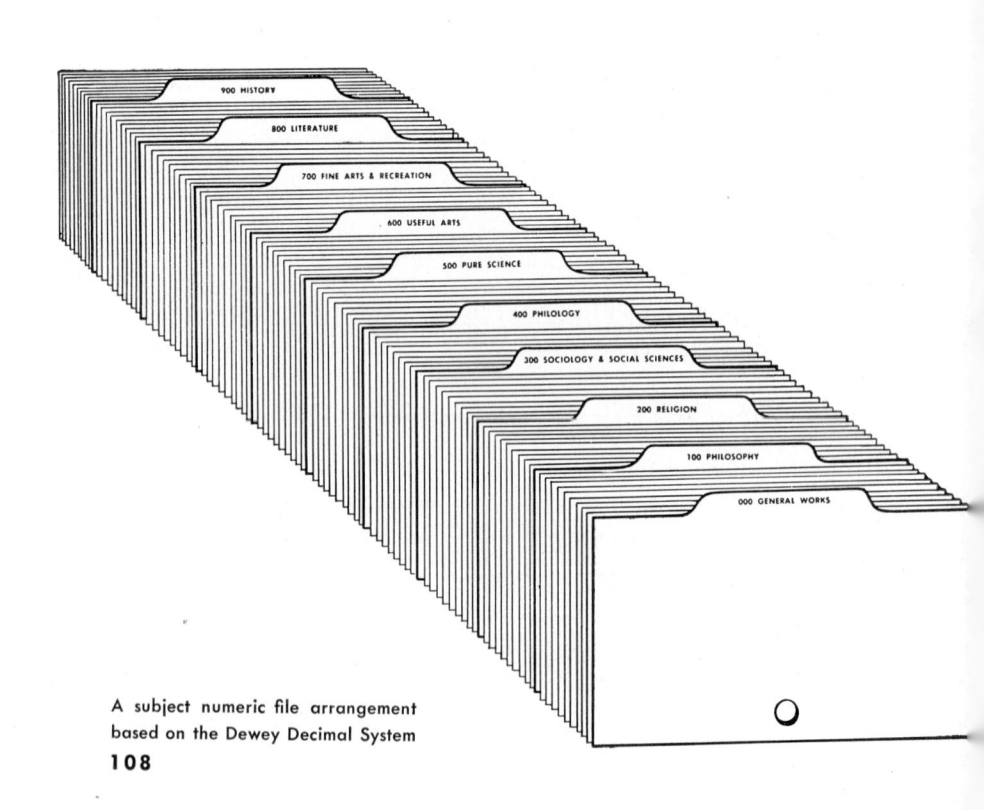

A subject numeric file arrangement
based on the Dewey Decimal System

108

Main Headings of the Dewey Decimal Classification for Libraries	Main Headings of the Williams Decimal Classification for Railroads	Main Headings of the Decimal Classification Used by the U. S. War Dept.
000 General Works	000 General	000 General
100 Philosophy	100 Executive and Legal	100 Finance and Accounting
200 Religion	200 Finance and Accounts	200 Personnel
300 Sociology	300 Roadways and Structures	300 Administration
400 Philology	400 Equipment and Shops	400 Supplies, Services, and Equipment
500 Natural Science	500 Transportation and Storage	500 Transportation
600 Useful Arts	600 Traffic, Rates	600 Buildings and Grounds
700 Fine Arts	700 Not assigned	700 Medicine, Hygiene, and Sanitation
800 Literature	800 Not assigned	800 Rivers, Harbors, and Waterways
900 History	900 Local Facilities and Affairs	900 Not assigned

ject, a decimal system of assigning numbers, based on the principle of the Dewey Decimal Classification used in libraries, may be used. According to this principle, papers are grouped under one of ten main headings, numbered in sequence in hundreds from 000 to 900 inclusive. The main heading numbered 000 is for papers too general or too inclusive in nature to be placed in any one of the other nine groups. In a library, dictionaries and encyclopedias are grouped in the 000 classification. Each of these main headings may be divided into nine or less divisions; for example, the main heading 200 could be divided into groups numbered 210, 220, 230, 240, 250, 260, 270, 280, and 290. These divisions could be further subdivided, if necessary, into nine or less first-subdivisions; for example, the 230 group could be divided into 231, 232, 233, 234, 235, 236, 237, 238, and 239. If further subdividing is necessary, a decimal point is placed and numbers added in sequence; for example, the 231 first-subdivision could be further subdivided into second-subdivisions numbered 231.1, 231.2, 231.3, 231.4, 231.5, 231.6, 231.7, 231.8, 231.9.

Decimal systems are found generally in libraries, railroads, public utilities, large engineering companies, and government bureaus. The table on page 109 compares the main headings of a decimal subject classification in three different fields. The illustration on page 108 will show the arrangement of guides and folders in a decimal system.

Other systems involving compound numeric notations are available. These systems are called duplex-numeric systems. In them, main headings are numbered in sequence with no regard to alphabetic arrangement. Divisions of the main headings would also be numbered in sequence, using a hyphen to indicate auxiliary numbers. For example, divisions of main heading 2 would be indicated by 2-1, 2-2, 2-3, etc. Each division could be further subdivided with the addition of more auxiliary numbers. For example, the third division of main group 2 could be subdivided into 2-3-1, 2-3-2, 2-3-3, 2-3-4, etc. Some people prefer to use letters after the first subdivision to eliminate the need for the hyphen. In other words, 3-1-1 could be designated 3-1a; and 3-1b could be used in place of 3-1-2. With the duplex-numeric systems, the number of main headings does not have to be limited to ten as in a decimal system. As a new main heading develops, the next unused number is simply assigned to it. The illustration below shows the arrangement of guides and folders in a duplex-numeric system.

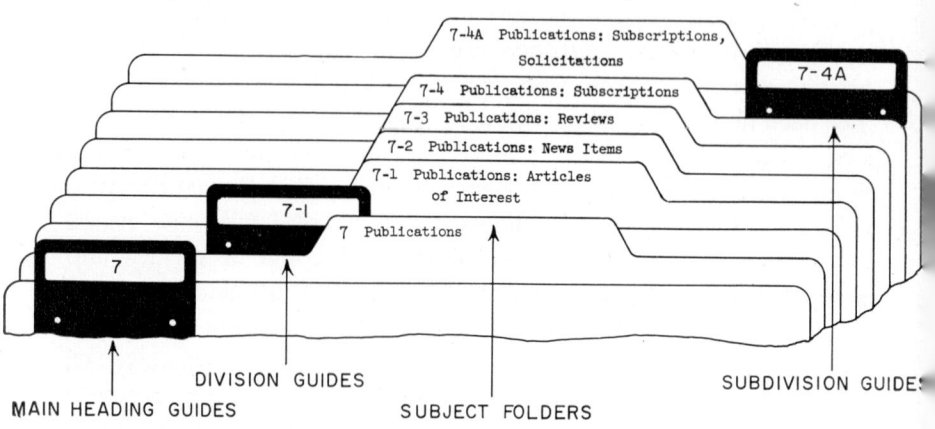

Arrangement of a duplex-numeric subject file

Subject Filing Procedure

The steps to be performed are quite similar to those followed in alphabetic filing.

Inspecting. Each paper should be checked to make sure it has been released for filing.

Indexing and coding. In a subject-alphabetic system, the paper may be coded by underlining the subject selected, if that subject corresponds in wording to the folder caption. In most cases, however, it is necessary to write the subject classification in the upper right-hand corner. In subject-numeric systems, the papers are coded by marking the folder number in the upper right-hand corner.

Many pieces of correspondence concern more than one subject and can be referred to under any one of them. The document itself should be filed under the most important subject and cross-referenced under the other subjects. The main heading, division, and subdivision, if any, under which the paper is actually filed are listed on the lower part of the cross-reference sheet. The cross-referenced main heading, division, and subdivision, if any, are written at the top of the cross-reference sheet. The cross-reference sheet illustrated on page 35 shows that a letter from the *Center Garage* was filed in the *Automobile Tires* folder, because the most important topic of the letter was automobile tires; however, the cross-reference sheet was placed in the *Bicycle Tires* folder because this subject was also discussed in the letter.

Sorting. The coded material is sorted first by the main headings, whether they are alphabetic or numeric. Then these piles are further sorted according to the divisions of the main heading and then by subdivisions.

Filing. Arrange all papers in a folder with the latest date to the front or on top.

QUESTIONS

for Review and Discussion

1. What is subject filing?
2. What are other names for a subject file?
3. When are subject files used?
4. Why is subject filing not so simple as alphabetic, geographic, or numeric?
5. If there are few papers to be filed by subject, how may they be handled?

4. Why is subject filing not so simple as alphabetic, geographic, or numeric?
5. If there are few papers to be filed by subject, how may they be handled?
6. What are the two main types of subject files?
7. What is the purpose of a subject classification? of a relative index?
8. What criteria should be used in selecting main headings and subdivisions in a subject filing system?
9. Describe one possible arrangement of guides and folders in a subject-alphabetic file.
10. When is a subject-numeric system usually used?
11. Describe the Dewey Decimal System.
12. Describe the duplex-numeric system.
13. How are papers coded in subject filing?
14. How are papers cross-referenced in subject filing?
15. How are papers sorted in subject filing?
16. How are papers arranged in a subject file folder.

Card and Visible Records

Nature of Card Systems

Card indexes are used in two ways—as auxiliary sources of information to be used along with some system of filing correspondence, or as independent means of obtaining or recording information. New developments in card-index equipment have increased the second use greatly.

For the most part, card indexes are used to record information that otherwise would have to be written in the form of a list in a bound or loose-leaf book. Information is easier to locate when the information is organized in card form, because each separate item is listed on its own card. Furthermore, a card system is more flexible: information may be changed by simply adding or removing cards without affecting other items, as might happen were the information in book form. Because of these characteristics, card systems are used extensively today for maintaining purchase records, sales records, inventory records, personnel records, payroll records, and bookkeeping ledger cards.

Card indexes, like correspondence files, may be organized on an alphabetic, geographic, subject, or numeric basis. However, each name, item, or subject must be listed on a separate card, so that it can be filed

Illustration courtesy New York Times

PROGRESSIVE FILING

Telephone inquiries about a customer's credit can be answered quickly if the information is kept on cards.

in the sequence demanded by the system adopted. To insure not only the accurate and rapid filing of information, but also the finding of it, the use of guides, one for every 25 to 50 cards, is a necessity. The standard sizes of cards are 5- by 3-inches, 6- by 4-inches, and 8- by 5-inches. The side the card rests on when filed is the first dimension given. The size of the card adopted must be determined by the amount of information to be placed on the cards. It is just as extravagant to choose too good or heavy a card as it is to choose a card that is too light in weight. It is not economy to put permanent records on inferior cards. The price of the best cards made is only a small fraction of the cost of putting the records on those cards. To buy cards that will last only a part of the life of the record means not only the expense of new cards, when the first lot is worn out and the slower reference to bent and dog-eared

Ledger cards of depositors' accounts are filed by account numbers in a savings bank. The name and signature cards are in card files above the ledger cards.

cards, but also the much greater expense of writing the record over again. On the other hand, for a record that is temporary in character or constantly changing, it is an evident waste to pay an extra price for cards of great durability. Cards are available in four weights: light, medium, heavy, and extra heavy, and in various grades of sulphite or rag content. It is also possible to obtain cards in at least eight colors for classification purposes.

Typing Cards. Cards may be filed on edge in drawers or trays of the proper size for the card used, or they may be filed by visible methods. When preparing cards that are to be filed vertically in drawers, the caption should be typed on the second line space from the top of the card. All additional key information should be kept as close as possible to the caption, so that it may be read without removing the card from the file. When preparing cards to be filed by visible methods, place the information as close to the lower edge of the card as possible.

Visible Records

As the name implies, a visible system enables the indexing information to be seen at all times. It permits faster location of information, because quite often it is unnecessary to handle the records as would be the case if they were filed on edge in card trays or drawers. Furthermore, visible records make signaling easier. As can be seen from the illustration below, various classifications of information can be indicated by the position or color, or both, of insert slips or signal tabs. Such signaling makes important facts stand out and safeguards the taking of appropriate action.

Three types of visible card-record files

All visible records belong to one of two types—the posted-record type, where information is being written continually on the card; and the index type, where nothing further has to be written once the information has been recorded. The index type is used for reference purposes only. All visible-record equipment—whether in the form of cabinets, books, or trays—can be obtained in two general styles, protected and unprotected, to take care of both the posted and reference type of records. Protected equipment is that style in which each record card is placed in a holder having a transparent covering at the indexing edge. It is used for either reference type or posting type of record. The posted type of record is usually housed in unprotected equipment to eliminate the need for removing the card from, and returning it to, the holder every time information has to be added. The specific needs of the business as to volume, place of use, portability, and type of use should be considered in deciding whether to select visible equipment in cabinet, rotary, book, tray, or tube form. Various types are illustrated on page 85 of Chapter 7 on Equipment and Supplies and on the facing page of this chapter.

Commercial Card Systems

In correspondence filing, special systems may be constructed to meet the needs of the particular organization; or various patented systems can be purchased. Manufacturers have adapted their patented correspondence systems for use in card filing.

In most file systems, names are filed as spelled. It is estimated that over 100,000 surnames can be spelled in from 2 to 20 different ways. For example, the surname *Burke* can be spelled many different ways, such as: *Berc, Berck, Berke, Birk, Birke, Borque, Bork, Bourke, Burk,* and *Burque*. These versions of the same name might be thousands of cards apart in a straight alphabetic file, and it would be difficult to find the correct card if it were not known which spelling was to be used. The correct spelling might not be known because the request for information came over the telephone or because of indistinct writing.

Soundex, a card system manufactured by Remington Rand, eliminates such difficulties because it is a "group name" system of indexing that brings all names that sound alike, but may be spelled differently,

Soundex takes care of the Burkes.

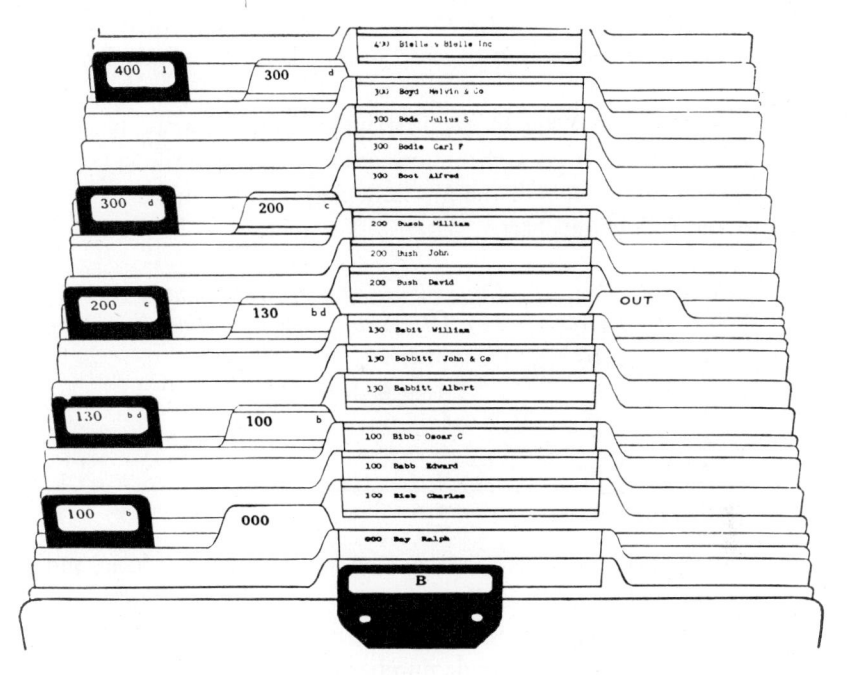

A file arranged according to Soundex

into one place in the file. It is based on the principle that certain key letters in the alphabet cannot be eliminated from a proper name without making it into something else. For example, eliminate *n* from *Snyder* and the name is changed to *Syder*. This method of filing is especially helpful in hospitals, banks, insurance companies, and government offices. The Social Security Department of the Federal Government uses this system, and it is said that any card can be located from the millions filed there within a minute.

Rules for Coding in a Soundex System

1 A Soundex file is divided into main sections, each guided by a letter of the alphabet, as, *A*, *B*, through *Z*. The first letter of the first indexing unit of a name determines the main alphabetic section in which it should be filed and is not coded. For example, according to the basic indexing rules, *James Himler* would be filed in the *H* main alphabetic section, because *Himler* is the first indexing

unit. The name *Boston Card Company* would be filed in the *B* main alphabetic section because *Boston* is the first indexing unit.

2 After the first letter in the first indexing unit has been used to determine the main alphabetic section, the next three key letters or their equivalents of the first indexing unit are coded according to the following chart.

Code No.	Key Letter	Equivalents—letters represented by the key letters because of sound similarity
1	b	p, f, v
2	c	s, k, g, j, q, x, z
3	d	t
4	l	—
5	m	n
6	r	—

Note: (1) The vowels *a, e, i, o, u* and the consonants *h, w,* and *y* are not coded, and are disregarded. (2) The code number consists of three digits—no more and no less. Zeros are added, if necessary, to make the code number three digits wide.

Example 1 The card pertaining to the *Dodson Art Shop* would be coded *D325*. *Dodson* is the first indexing unit according to the basic indexing rules; and *D* is the first letter of that unit, so the card would be filed in the *D* main alphabetic section of the file. The first letter of the first indexing unit having been used for selecting the main alphabetic section of the file is *not* given a code number. The second letter is the vowel *o*, which is disregarded. The next letter is *d*, which is assigned the code number *3;* the next letter is *s* which is coded *2;* the next letter is *o* and is disregarded; and the next letter is *n*, which is assigned the code number *5*.

Example 2 The card pertaining to *John Slakerman* would be coded *S426*. *Slakerman* is the first indexing unit according to the basic indexing rules; and *S* is the first letter of that unit, so the card would be filed in the *S* main alphabetic section of the file. The first letter of the first indexing unit having been used for selecting the main alphabetic section of the file is *not* given a code number. The second letter is *l*, which is assigned the code number *4;* the next letter, *a*, is disregarded; the next letter, *k*, is assigned code number *2;* the next letter, *e*, is disregarded; and the next letter, *r*, is assigned code number *6.* Because each code number must consist of not more than *3* numbers, the rest of the name is disregarded.

Example 3   The card pertaining to the *John Bird Company* would be coded *B630*. B, the first letter of the first indexing unit, decides that the card will be filed in the *B* main alphabetic section. The next letter, *i*, is disregarded; the *r* is assigned number *6;* and the last letter, *d*, is assigned number *3.* Since only two digits have been assigned, and each code number should have three, a zero is added to complete the number.

Example 4   *Siegal, Siegel, Segal, Siegle*—coded *240* in the *S* section.

Example 5   *Headley, Hedley, Hudley, Hutley*—coded *340* in the *H* section.

Example 6   *Bunson, Benson, Bunsen*—coded *525* in the *B* section.

Example 7   *Rex, Reks*—coded *200* in the *R* section.

Example 8   *Marshall, Marchall, Marschal*—coded *624* in the *M* section.

3   When two or more *consecutive* letters are represented by the same key letter, code them as one letter. In other words, only the first of those consecutive letters represented by the same key letter is considered; the others are disregarded.

Example 1   *Hardtmann* is coded *635* (*r-6, d-3, m-5*) in the *H* section. The *d* and *t* are represented by the same key letter *d*. Therefore the *t* is disregarded.

Example 2   Jackson is coded *250* (*c-2, n-5*) in the *J* section. The *J* is disregarded because it was the initial letter of the unit used to identify the main filing section. The *c*, *k*, and *s* occur together and are represented by the same key letter; therefore, the *k* and *s* are disregarded. The *n* is represented by the *5*, and a zero is added to fill out the code number to three digits.

Example 3 *Lloyd* is coded *300* (*d-3*) in the *L* section. The two *l's* occur together and have the same key letter; therefore, according to the rule, the second *l* is disregarded. But in this case the first *l* is also disregarded, because it has already been used to designate the main filing section. *O* and *Y* are disregarded; *d* is coded *3;* and two zeros are added to fill the code number out to three digits.

Example 4 *Schneider* is coded *536* (*n-5, d-3, r-6*) in the *S* section. The *S* and *c* occur together and are represented by the same key letter, therefore the *c* is disregarded. The *S* is also disregarded, because it was the initial letter of the unit used to identify the main filing section.

4 If two letters represented by the same key letter are separated by *a, e, i, o, u,* or *y*, the two letters are coded *separately*. If, however, two letters represented by the same key letter are separated by *h* or *w*, the second of the letters represented by the same key is disregarded.

Example 1 *Newman* is coded *550* (*m-5, n-5*) in the *N* section. *N*, the first key letter, is used to designate the main alphabetic section. The letters *e* and *w* are disregarded. The next letter, *m*, is coded *5;* the next letter, *a*, is disregarded; and the next letter, *n*, although represented by the same key letter as *m*, is coded also because the two letters are separated by *a*.

Example 2 *Ashcroft* is coded *261* (*s-2, r-6, f-1*) in the *A* section. *A*, the first key letter, is used to designate the main alphabetic section. The letter *s* is assigned code number *2; h* is disregarded; *c* is also disregarded, because it has the same key letter as *s*, and the two letters are separated by *h*.

5 The coded first indexing unit of the name decides what guide the card will follow. All cards behind any one guide are arranged alphabetically according to the *second* indexing units. If the second indexing units are alike, the third must be considered. For example, the card for *Frank J. Smith* would be filed behind the 530 guide of the *S* division and would be behind the *Frank D. Smyth* card but ahead of the *Fred Smith* card.

QUESTIONS

for Review and Discussion

1. In what two ways are card indexes used?
2. What are the advantages of listing information on cards?
3. Name four ways of organizing card indexes.
4. How many guides are needed in a card file?
5. What are the standard sizes of file cards?
6. What determines the quality of the card to be used?
7. How may cards be filed?
8. What are the advantages of visible records?
9. What are the two types of visible records?
10. What two general styles of visible-file equipment are available?
11. What is Soundex?

Chapter 12

Establishing and Maintaining Filing Systems

Fitting the System to the Needs

Filing experts can be called in to analyze existing filing systems or to make new installations. This type of service is provided by independent business consultants as well as by some of the manufacturers of filing equipment, supplies, and systems. Most large organizations find it advisable to avail themselves of such professional advice. The people in small offices who are responsible for the management of records can do likewise or, at least, analyze their own systems and procedures in the same general manner as the experts.

The front of the analysis sheet illustrated on page 126 is used by the experts of a well-known file-equipment company to study existing systems. The same basic facts, however, must be considered by everyone who is installing a new system or attempting to improve an old one to obtain the most efficient and economical filing service. These fundamental factors are:

1. What type of filing system should be used?
    (a) alphabetic, (b) numeric, (c) geographic, (d) subject
    (e) type and volume of material filed
    (f) how used and by whom
2. What kind of equipment and supplies should be used?
    (a) cabinets, (b) guides, (c) folders
3. What filing procedures should be used?
    (a) collection, (b) cross-referencing, (c) charge-out
    (d) follow-up, (e) sorting
4. What provision should be made for retention?
    (a) transfer plan, (b) transfer equipment and where kept

Type of Filing System

A filing system, like bookkeeping, production, or any other system, must be tailored to the type of business and its needs. What information is needed for the efficient operation of the business? How will that information be used, and who will request it? The answers to these questions should determine the system to be used for filing the records.

Realizing that the material to be filed involves more than incoming mail and copies of outgoing letters, today's executives are consulting more and more with the person responsible for the files when a record or form is created. Standardization of size and of placement of data on forms facilitates the handling of records and speeds up the filing and finding of documents.

The files should not be a depository for every paper handled by an organization. Only those containing information that will be used should be retained. All organizations, large and small, should periodically analyze the number of times each type of record has been called from the files for use and by whom. On the basis of this experience, intelligent decisions can be made as to the advisability of continuing to file such records and in what way.

Two different departments or individuals might use the same record for different operations and therefore ask for that paper in different ways, such as by customer's name or by order number. Although some large organizations might organize separate files for each department,

RECORDS ANALYSIS WORK SHEET

COMPANY: XYZ Chemical Company
ADDRESS: 150 Springfield Ave., Quincy, Illinois
DATE: 3/25/55
DEPARTMENT: General Office
LOCATION OF RECORDS: Room 1609
INTERVIEWED: Jane Smith

TITLE – Full Description of File/Records: Correspondence, Reports, Maps, Photographs, and Source Material (Printed Data)

FILE SEQUENCE:
- Alphabetic ☑
- Numeric ☐
- Indexed By: ___

KIND OF FILE:
- Correspondence ☑
- Printed Forms ☐
- Printed Literature ☐
- Cards ☐
- Other (Explain) ☐

DOCUMENTATION:
- Incl. Dates: 1937-1955
- Condition: good
- Legibility: good
- Color: white   Size: 8½ × 11
- Kind of Paper: Bond
- Typed ☑   Hand written ☑
- One Side ☑   Both Sides ☐

PURPOSE: To service customers and Plant information.

FOLDERS
Made By: Remington Rand Inc.

Avg. No. per Drawer	No. per Guide	No. papers per Folder
500	50	10-100

- No. Active Names per Dwr.: 25   % Total ___
- No. Inactive Names per Dwr.: 75   % Total ___
- No. Folders with Exceptional Volume ___

Tab Cut	Tab Position
½	left and right

Type of Fasteners: Acco

Sequence of Papers in Folders: Chronological

Type of Miscellaneous Folders: Manila

Sequence of Papers in Misc. Folders: Chronological

GUIDES
Made By: Remington Rand Inc.

Average No. per Drawer: 10

Tab Cut: ½

Tab Position: left and right

Subdivisions:
Primary – Alphabetic
Secondary – Special name

Special Guides: none

FILE CABINETS: Wood ☐   Steel ☑
Made By: Remington Rand Inc.

Conditions: Cabinets ok.
Folders - written in ink and over crowded.

	No.	Ltr.	Leg.	How Full
4 Drawer	6	6	–	75-100 %
5 Drawer	–	–	–	

Transfer Cases: folding cartons & boxes

PROCEDURES (Explain)
Sorting: none

Cross-Reference: none

Charge-Out: none

Follow-up: none

Relative Index: none

Written Instructions: none

ACTIVITY
- No. Papers filed each day: 100   week: 500
- No. References each day: 15   week: 75
- File is Active ☐   Semi-Active ☐   Inactive ☑

RETENTION POLICY (Present)
- None ☐   Permanent ☐   Partial ☑
- Destroy after: not established.

TRANSFER PROCEDURE (Explain)
Maintain some subjects since 1937. Each January pulled from general file.

DUPLICATION of File/Papers? (Explain)
no

VALUE AND APPRAISAL (PROPOSED)
- Non-essential ☑   Destroy after 1 yr.   Important ☑   Destroy after study
- Useful ☑   Destroy after 3 yrs.   Vital (Permanent) ☐   Historical (Perm'nt) ☑

Basis for Appraisal:
Additional careful study required as to material which has permanent value and must be retained.

Other records no longer needed after one or two years should be destroyed.

There is some material which should be transferred for a period to be determined after evaluation.

Microfilm Applicable? (Explain):
Study maps and source material for possible filming.

A records analysis sheet (front)

obviously this would be more expensive in terms of the filing space needed, the number of copies made, and the labor needed for filing than the maintaining of one centralized filing department for all operations. Generally the filing arrangement adopted should be the one that permits the fastest location of a record for its most frequent user.

The following advantages and disadvantages of the various systems should be considered.

Alphabetic Filing

Advantages

1. Provides for the grouping of papers pertaining to the same individual or company.
2. Direct filing and reference. No index required.
3. Simplicity of guide and folder arrangement.
4. Provides for miscellaneous papers.

Disadvantages

1. Congestion under common names.
2. Possibility of filing related papers in more than one place because of variation in spelling surnames.

Geographic Filing

Advantages

1. Provides for grouping of papers by location.
2. Direct filing and reference.
3. Provides for miscellaneous papers.

Disadvantages

1. Sorting by territorial divisions and then by alphabetic order increases the possibility of error and raises labor cost.
2. Location as well as name must be known.
3. Need for occasional reference to card index.

Subject Filing

Advantages

1. Provides for grouping of papers by topics, to establish relationships of a statistical or technical nature.
2. Unlimited expansion.

Disadvantages

1. Difficulty in classifying papers for filing.
2. Need for liberal cross-referencing.
3. Unsatisfactory provision for miscellaneous papers.
4. Need for occasional reference to index to determine subject heading or subdivision.

Numeric Filing

Advantages	*Disadvantages*
1. Accuracy.	1. Indirect filing and reference.
2. Positive numbers that may be used to identify the name or subject when calling for correspondence. These same numbers may be used in various departments and files.	2. Separate file must be maintained for miscellaneous papers.
3. Unlimited expansion.	3. Cumbersome index.
4. Opportunity for permanent and liberal cross-referencing.	4. High labor cost.
5. Index is a complete list of names and addresses of all correspondents and subjects.	

Over 90 per cent of the filing systems in use are alphabetic systems. The simplest kind, and of course the most widely used in point of quantity, is a one- or two-drawer file with a separate guide for each letter of the alphabet. These simple systems satisfy the needs of thousands of small business and professional people. In many instances, such files are adequate for individual executive files and for small departmental units in larger businesses. Provision can also be made in these simple alphabetic systems for folders for common subjects as well as for the active correspondents and miscellaneous material. The adopted system should be accurate, speedy, and flexible to provide for growth in the business.

Kind of Equipment and Supplies

One of the reasons why filing is sometimes unpopular with the people in small offices who are responsible for that activity, in addition to other duties, is that their filing equipment does not permit good housekeeping. Modern kitchens are planned to save steps, provide adequate space, and encourage neatness. Similar thought should be given to the location and procurement of filing equipment. File cabinets contain records too important to be buried in basements, corridors, or back rooms. If they are kept in a position closest to the point of use, much working fatigue can be eliminated; and the tendency to procrastinate on filing can be discouraged. Even in the smallest office, careful planning can get the file cabinets closer to you.

A convenient desk-drawer file

Open-Shelf Files. Open-shelf files are becoming increasingly popular for the filing of both active and inactive records. They save up to 50 per cent of floor space, because the space needed for the opening of file drawers is eliminated; and shelving may be seven or eight shelves high. They also save 75 per cent of the cost of first-grade filing cabinets; moreover, filed material is more easily accessible. Because of these qualifications, open-shelf files are recommended for very large and active files away from the public view as well as for transferred records. Special guides and folders with tabs on the end are available for open-shelf systems, and color devices have been developed as safeguards against misfiling.

Types of Cabinets. If your filing-space needs are small, perhaps a desk-drawer file or a movable tray, which can be relocated when necessary, might help. Cabinets, desk high to give extra work surface, or cabinets, counter high that can act as partitions and yet provide working surface, might be the answer.

Not only must the cabinets be properly located to reduce fatigue, but there must be sufficient space within each drawer. Drawers filled to overflowing require extra time and energy to remove and replace folders, not to mention the additional wear and tear on important papers, guides, and folders. Then too, you are psychologically encouraged to work at a neat, roomy drawer, while a crammed one repels

130 | PROGRESSIVE FILING

you. Leave approximately four inches of operating space within each file drawer. When purchasing your cabinets, plan for future requirements as well as present needs and remember the files should fit the system, not the system the files.

Each drawer should be conspicuously and specifically labeled so that the contents can be identified speedily without necessitating the opening of the drawer. Either single or double captions may be used; however, the double captions have the advantage of giving the range of contents, whereas with single captions the labels on two drawers must be scanned. The conventional way of using file drawers is from top to bottom as in the illustration at the left on page 131, although some authorities say it is easier to work from side to side if there are adjacent

A section of an open-shelf file

cabinets as in the illustration at the right shown below.

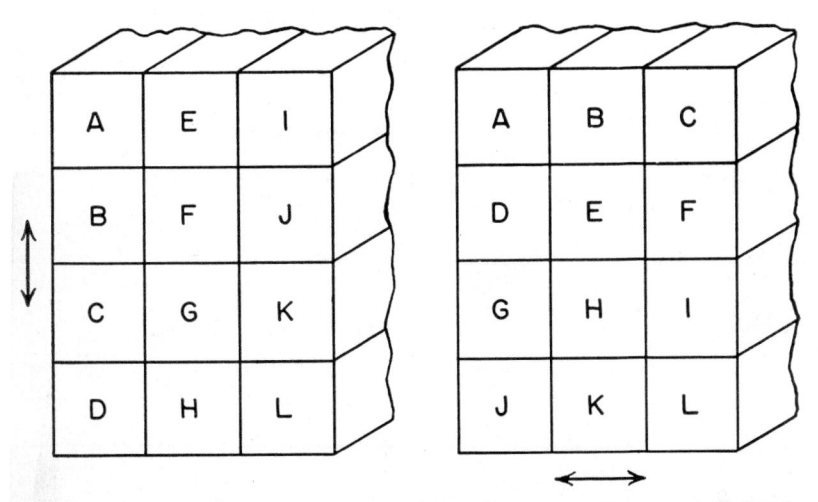

Your filing-guide requirements will be in proportion to the amount of drawer space you use. The usual number of guides in each drawer should be between 20 and 40, in order to provide proper distribution of papers, to facilitate reference, and to furnish support.

Remington-Rand suggests the following proportion of guides to drawer space and correspondence.

Drawers of Correspondence	Number of Pieces Filed	Alphabetic Index Required
1	up to 4,000	20–40
2	4,000–6,000	40–60
3	6,000–8,000	60–80
4	8,000–10,000	80–100
5–6	10,000–15,000	100–150
7–8	15,000–20,000	150–200
9–12	20,000–30,000	200–300
13–16	30,000–40,000	300–400
17–20	40,000–50,000	400–500
21–24	50,000–60,000	500–600
25–28	60,000–80,000	600–800
29–36	80,000–100,000	800–1,000

Whatever arrangement of guides you select should be flexible enough to permit your files to grow without necessitating the discarding of present guides or folders and without interfering with the smooth

132 | PROGRESSIVE FILING

operation of your system. Notice in the following illustration how easily a 150 guide set was expanded to a 200 guide set by the simple addition of specific subdivisions.

TODAY...

TOMORROW...

The average number of folders filed behind any one guide should be from 5 to 10. To keep the files neat and workable and to afford a maximum of protection to the papers, the folders should not be allowed to become too bulky. Standard-size folders will hold 100 sheets of paper and stand up. Beyond 100 sheets, the folder curls down in the drawer, and the tabs become hidden and difficult to read. When correspondence nears this volume, a new folder should be started basing the separation on either date, or location, or subject. If it is necessary that all the correspondence pertaining to one correspondent or subject be kept in one folder and the amount of this correspondence is too great for a standard-size folder, a heavy pressboard expansion folder, or envelope, or binder folder may be used.

Papers may be permitted to accumulate in a miscellaneous folder until there are five or more about one correspondent or subject; then an individual folder can be started for the name. Within individual folders, papers are arranged by date, the latest date being to the front of the folder or on top. Within miscellaneous folders, papers are arranged alphabetically; if two or more papers pertain to the same name, the paper with the latest date is placed on top.

Special follow-up folders, signal devices, colored inserts, and labels, described in Chapter 7 on Selection of Equipment and Supplies, can be used as reminders to attract the eye to folders that require special attention.

Attention to Filing Procedures

There are more misplaced papers in small offices, in proportion to the volume handled, than in large organizations. At first this is difficult to understand when you consider that the chances for error are greater in a large organization where more papers are handled and more people are involved. However, the realization of this error possibility causes the large organizations to give adequate attention to the important aspects of filing routine, with a resulting increase in speed and accuracy of filing. Too often in a small office, a necessary filing procedure is neglected or dismissed with the statement, "That's all right for a large office, but we're too small to need it." What is good filing routine for a large organization is also good routine for a small office. The routine may be modified or less formal in a small office, but certainly none of the essential phases should be omitted.

In many small offices, the search for needed papers resembles a constant "treasure hunt" that starts with the files and then branches out into the desk trays and drawers of the workers' desks. This happens because mail does not get into the files within a reasonable time after it is received or is not returned to the files promptly after being borrowed. Most large organizations require that all incoming mail be stamped to show the date and time of arrival and that it be answered or other appropriate action taken within a set time. In a small office, possibly the time-stamping can be dispensed with, but certainly the secretary should check the boss's "to-be-handled" tray every day to make sure he is not using it as an accumulating receptacle. By so stimulating your boss into action, you will be keeping the people happy with whom you do business, and at the same time will be getting papers into the safekeeping of the file where they are easier to locate.

Large organizations require that whenever a paper is removed from the files, regardless of who does it (even the boss) or for how long, a charge-out guide, folder, or substitution card must be inserted in its place. This guide, folder, or card shows the name of the person using the paper, the date of removal, a description of the paper, and other pertinent information if needed. Possibly all this written information is not needed in the small office, but certainly the charge-out guide or folder should still be inserted when material is removed. That charge-out makes it so much easier for you in three ways: first, it tells you that material is being used so that you do not think it has been lost or misfiled; second, it enables you to follow up the borrowed material to make sure it gets back to the files; third, it makes it so simple to find the proper place when the material is finally returned to the files. By all means, if you are or will be a small-office worker, keep a supply of charge-out guides or folders in the front or back of *every* file drawer, so that they are conveniently located and like a bookmark can be popped into place when needed. See illustrations of charge-out guides on page 65.

Large organizations place a restriction on the length of time papers may be borrowed from the files, so that other would-be users will not be kept waiting and also to reduce chances of loss. If the material is not returned on the due date, the user is requested to return it or to reborrow it. The small office does not have so great a problem of sharing the filed papers among the workers; but because no one person has been hired as a file worker exclusively, there is the tendency to allow papers to accumulate in desk trays or drawers. The longer papers remain out of the files, the greater the likelihood of loss! It is so easy and takes so little time in the small office with its few file drawers to glance through them just before quitting time every night, to note what material is out, as indicated by the out guides, folders, or cards; and then to follow up the borrower to ascertain if he has finished with it.

Few people enjoy washing, drying, or putting away dishes. Yet if dishes are taken care of immediately after each meal, the chore is not too burdensome. But if the dishes are permitted to accumulate until there is a considerable number to be handled, the task becomes disturbing, both mentally and physically. The people in small offices who say they dislike filing are the ones who, like the dishwasher, let the task get out of hand. Because filing is an incidental activity, they perform other more frequently occurring duties. As the papers to be filed pile up higher and higher, the temptation to put off the filing becomes greater and greater. It is a mistake in a small office to postpone regular filing of papers, because only a few have to be put away. Psychologically, it is wise; and practically, it is a "must" to get those papers into the files without delay where they are safe and the information they supply is available rapidly.

One short cut to filing speed in all offices, large and small, is the performing of two operations simultaneously. To complete the indexing and coding of all papers to be filed before doing the preliminary sorting would require two handlings of the same papers; however, placing each paper in the proper group immediately after it is indexed and coded would require that it be handled only once. Sorting can be performed on desk tops without using any of the special sorting equipment described in Chapter 7 on Equipment and Supplies. Special equipment, however, does get the sorting done faster and with less effort. It organizes the work more efficiently and prevents papers from being scattered by electric fans or suddenly opened doors or windows, as can happen with desk-top sorting. Furthermore, the sorting equipment does save stops and starts for the crisscrossing or rubber-banding of items, because all papers are held firmly in position by dividers in the units. See illustrations of sorting equipment on pages 34 and 38.

When placing the sorted papers in the files, work from the side of the drawer, not the front. From the side position, the worker does not have to reach as far, thus reducing fatigue of the arms and neck. Proper lighting over the files will reduce eyestrain and error. Always pull up any folder in which papers are to be filed. This practice prevents papers from slipping between folders and falling to the bottom of the drawer where they are lost. Avoid the use of paper clips. They not only hold together the papers you want grouped, but sometimes latch on to papers that are not related; furthermore, they add to the bulk of the file. Staples are to be preferred for fastening purposes. When a paper or a folder is removed from the drawer to be returned *immediately*, slightly lift the paper or folder behind the one removed to make it easier to locate the place of return. Of course, if the material is not to be returned immediately, an out card, folder, or guide is used.

Even in the best-managed files, the human element causes an occasional error. If a paper is not where you first look, don't let panic take hold of you, but organize your search along the following lines.

1. Make sure the paper is not misplaced in the proper folder, or is not sticking to some other paper in that folder.
2. Look in the desk trays. Possibly someone removed it for use and forgot to insert an out guide.
3. Look in the folders just in *front* and *behind* the proper folder.
4. Look in the *space* just in front, behind, and under the proper folder.
5. If you are using an alphabetic name system, look under similar names —first those that have similar spelling, and then if you had no luck, those that are similar as to sound.
6. If you are using an alphabetic name system, try the other indexing units. Possibly it was filed under the second or third unit instead of the first.
7. If you are using an alphabetic name or subject system, try to think of some *related* name or topic under which it could have been filed even though it is not cross-referenced.
8. If you are using a numeric system, try every possible arrangement of the correct folder number. If the correct number is *3892*, try *3892, 3829, 8392, 8329*, etc.

If you finally locate the missing paper, take steps, if possible, to remove the cause of error. If the missing paper is not located, either insert a replica of it, or a notification of its loss so that a needless search is not made again if the paper is requested subsequently.

Provision for Retention

Few filing systems are, or should be, set up to retain material indefinitely. One of the transfer methods discussed in Chapter 6 that best fits the needs of your organization must be selected. However, the work of the transfer operation can be reduced and speeded up by combining a part of it with another filing operation. Ordinarily at transfer time, before the material can be physically transferred or destroyed, a decision must be made as to what should be kept and for how long. Arriving at that decision is the most difficult part of the transfer operation and quite a responsibility for the file worker. Many organizations, however, make the decision as to the period of retention at the time the material is first released for filing. Instead of simply initialing in the upper right-hand corner to give the authority to file, the receiver of the document releases it by indicating in the upper right-hand corner how long it should be kept in the active files and whether or not after that period it should be transferred or destroyed.

Releasing material for the files in this fashion not only puts the decision on the shoulders of the person best qualified to make it, but also speeds up the actual transfer operation.

Memory Helpers

Have you ever envied the people who seem to have good memories? More than likely their memories are no better than yours, but they have the secret of not cluttering their minds with details. They put information they are likely to forget on paper and study up on it just prior to the time of use.

Those politicians or important executives who flatter "little you" by remembering you and the conditions under which you met more than likely maintain a name file. It works something like this. Information about a person is recorded in three places—under the name of the individual, under the name of the organization with which he is connected, and under the name of the city where the organization is located. Then if "Mr. Big" plans a trip to Dallas, just before he leaves, he has his secretary bring the *Dallas* folder to him, and he studies up on the people there whom he might meet again. Or if he is to have a meeting with the XYZ Corporation, a few minutes with the name folder of that organization and he will know the names of the officers and important executives and other pertinent data. Of course, if he knows he is to meet a certain person, that individual's folder or card will do the memory refreshing.

If your boss has occasion to meet many people and you want to get him in the proper frame of mind for your next salary-increase request, suggest some such system to him. It does call for co-operation on his part, but it only takes a few minutes after his attendance at a meeting or an affair for him to jot down the names of the people he met and pertinent information, such as E. G. Smith, president of Fido Dog Biscuits—likes cigars; Bill Jones, credit manager of Elkton Company—good golf player.

Another way to make a hit with a busy employer is to give him a list of his next day's appointments just before he leaves the office each evening. This reminder can be placed on 5-by-3 cards and will enable him to plan his activities.

PROGRESSIVE FILING

In every office, certain things have to be done at certain times. Because it is unwise to depend on the human memory, some reminder system should be used. These mechanical memories are called many names, some of which are: follow-up file, tickler file, suspense file, pending file, HFA (hold for answer) file. The systems also vary somewhat in method depending on the size and needs of the business organization. However, they are all essentially date files.

The simplest reminder system and one with which everyone is familiar is the desk calendar pad. By merely turning to the proper page you can list the appointment or activity that must be remembered for that particular day. The calendar pad gives a complete picture of the day's activities but because of its space limitations cannot be used where a large number of notations have to be made. Moreover, it is a "personal" book and would not be satisfactory where many people have to refer to the follow-up information.

A card follow-up system, like the one illustrated on page 64, can be expanded to handle an unlimited amount of information. It consists of twelve month guides, a set of 1-31 date guides for the current month, and a desk tray. These guides are arranged with the current-month guide in the front, followed by the date guides, which in turn are followed by the remaining month guides in sequence. Whenever a matter needs future attention, the name of the person or subject involved, the date, and other necessary facts are listed on a 5-by-3 card. This card is then filed behind the guide showing the date when the matter must be taken up. If it is a matter that will take considerable work, be sure to enter it, not on the date it must be done, but sufficiently in advance to allow ample time for its completion.

Each morning the reminder cards for that day should be removed from the file. The date guide is then placed behind the guide for the next month, thereby getting the next month ready for day-by-day division. Then, whatever the cards call for should be done—the Jones invoice paid in order to qualify for the discount, your boss told that the price quotations the Smith Company had promised within a period of ten days had not arrived, the insurance policy on the company trucks renewed.

Some office workers like two sets of date guides—one for the current month and the other for the succeeding month—but this is not necessary, unless there is a heavy volume of follow-up material. There is a clever device that some people use to avoid listing matters for follow-up on days that the office is closed. They either reverse the date guide so the blank side shows or they remove the guide entirely from the current month. The reminder cards for that particular date are filed behind the preceding day's guide.

In a large organization with a central filing department, a sheet tickler system may sometimes be used to advantage. As in the card tickler method, a set of month guides and a set of date guides are used. However, they are correspondence size and are kept in a regular correspondence-size drawer. When it is known that some matter discussed in an *outgoing* letter will require follow-up, an extra carbon copy is prepared. The usual carbon is sent to the central filing department while the extra copy is placed behind the proper date in the tickler file. When an *incoming* letter is received that will require future attention, a substitution card is made out listing briefly the required data. The letter itself is then sent to the central files, while the substitution card is placed behind the proper date in the tickler. On the date the letter is again needed, the substitution card is sent to the central file department. It is inserted in the folder in place of the letter to show where the actual letter is. The original letter then comes back to the person who needs it for follow-up purposes. Such a system guarantees that the November 12 letter from the ABC Company will be located where workers from the Sales Department, the Accounting Department, the Collection Department, or any other department will have ready access to it if necessary. Yet it provides the needed information for reminding someone to follow it up on December 2.

In some situations, a combination alphabetic and date file will be best for follow-up purposes. This method works well in small personal files or where some of the pending papers have no specific follow-up date. As many alphabetic guides as are deemed necessary may be used. In back of each alphabetic guide there are two date guides—one bearing the notation *1-14* and the other *15-31*. Papers *with* specific follow-up dates are filed without folders behind the correct alphabetic and date guide. Papers *without* specific follow-up dates are filed in individual name or subject folders arranged alphabetically behind the guides.

Special supplies, illustrated on page 141, can be used advantageously

140 | PROGRESSIVE FILING

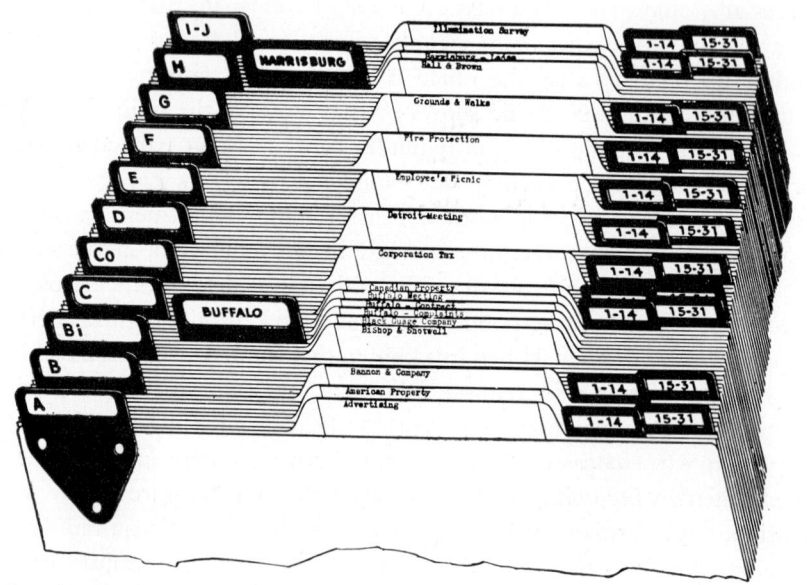

A combination alphabetic and date file

to help in locating the information needed in follow-up systems. There are date folders that have a straight top edge sheathed in transparent celluloid. The title is inserted under the celluloid on the left side. Printed under the celluloid to the right of the title space are the months of the year with the numbers *1-31*. By sliding a movable pointer to the proper place on the scale, a follow-up date can be indicated. Cards known as tab cards, because of the tab or projection on the upper edge, provide follow-up information by the position of the tab or the information printed on the tab or both. The projections on the tab card are part of the card and because of that are immovable. Metal signals are obtainable, however, which can be clamped on the top of cards or folders. They can be used to give information through position or color or both. They are more flexible than tab cards because a simple shift in color or position will make a change in classification that in a tab card arrangement might call for an entirely new card.

ESTABLISHING FILING SYSTEMS | 141

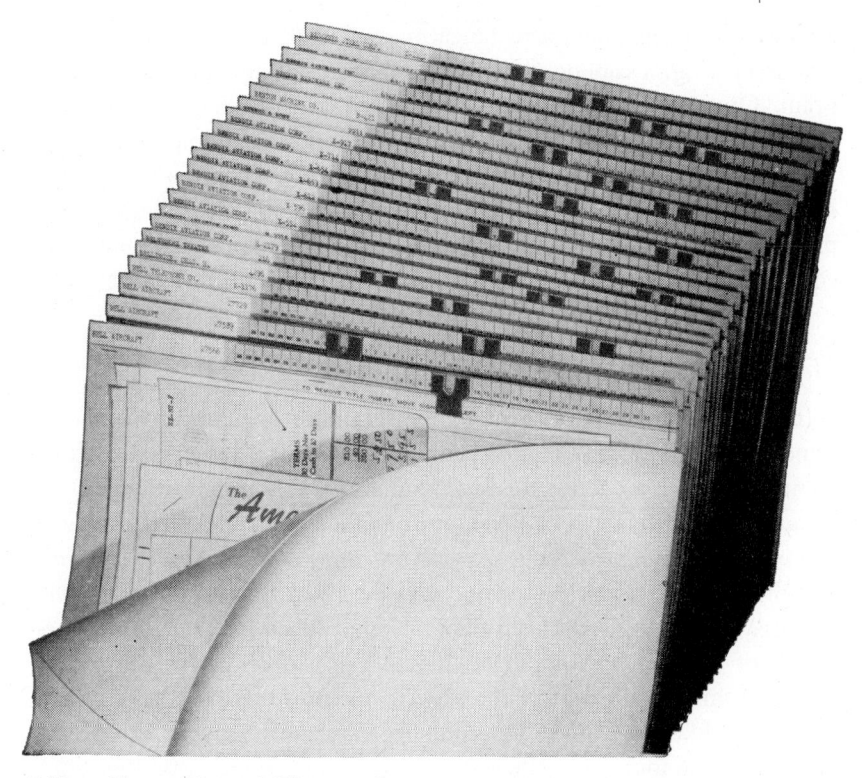

Folders with movable metal follow-up tabs

Most papers in the files are records of things that have already happened—incoming and outgoing letters; incoming and outgoing business forms; bookkeeping records of purchases, sales, and manufacturing; and reports and analyses of operations. However, a clever individual can also use the files in another way—it is sometimes called the library function—that is, for the purpose of compiling data that *might* be used at some future time in connection with a particular subject or subjects. Does your boss do quite a bit of public speaking? Get him and others to jot down on a piece of paper or card those hilarious jokes heard or read. The same can be done with outstanding speeches that are heard or magazine articles read that might suggest topics or material usable in future talks. This "getting ready" process can be applied to any topic related to individual or company activities—a newspaper clipping about a clever sales campaign, a technical magazine article on some phase of manufacturing, a catalogue of office supplies, an ingenious dinner program. Obviously, discretion must be used in selecting what to save; only outstanding material for the most important topics, otherwise your files will be bulging in no time at all. However, properly applied, accumulating information in advance of the time of use will ultimately produce a better end result with far less effort. Special supplies and equipment are available to help house clippings and catalogues.

Getting Expert Advice

It is all right in the case of minor scratches or aches to use home remedies or first aid, but most people wisely go to a doctor for treatment of everything above this level. Similarly, although many decisions about filing matters can be made by the office personnel, it is advisable to get the opinions of filing experts on important aspects of systems and procedures. Often the advice will be given free as a "good-will" gesture, so that you will keep them in mind when making future purchases of supplies or equipment. If it is a situation that calls for considerable time on the part of the expert, any consultation charge would more than likely be offset for your organization in a very short time because of the increased efficiency of the filing service.

QUESTIONS

for Review and Discussion

1. What fundamental factors must be considered in analyzing the effectiveness of a filing system?
2. Why should the person in charge of the files be consulted when a business form is created?
3. Why should all organizations periodically analyze the material that has been called from the files?
4. Why are departmentalized files usually more expensive to maintain than centralized files?
5. What are the advantages and disadvantages of alphabetic filing? of numeric filing? of geographic filing? of subject filing?

6. What type of filing is most common?
7. What should determine the location of filing cabinets?
8. What is open-shelf filing, and why is it used?
9. Why should drawers not be overfilled?
10. Compare the use of single and double captions for drawer labels.
11. How many guides are needed in a file drawer?
12. What is meant by "The guide arrangement should be flexible enough to allow for growth"?
13. Why should folders not be allowed to become too bulky?
14. What is the capacity of a standard-size folder?
15. When is an individual folder started?
16. How are papers arranged within an individual folder? within a miscellaneous folder?
17. Where is there generally a higher degree of filing accuracy—in large or small organizations? Why?
18. What are the advantages of the prompt collection of papers?
19. What are the advantages of using charge-out cards?
20. Is a follow-up system necessary in a small office? Why?
21. Even though the volume of papers is small, why is it unwise to postpone filing in a small office?
22. How does simultaneous coding and sorting save filing time and effort?
23. List some good practices to be followed when working at the file drawer.
24. Describe the procedure you would follow in looking for a missing paper.
25. Describe a technique for simplifying the transfer operation.
26. Explain how a "name memory" file works.
27. Give some other names for a follow-up file.
28. Explain how a follow-up file works.
29. How does a sheet-tickler system differ from a card tickler?
30. Illustrate what is meant by the library function of filing.

Summary of Rules

RULE

1. **Names of Individuals** Transpose the names of individuals. Consider the surname (last name) first, the given name (first name) second, and the middle name, if any, third.

2. **Alphabetic Order** Each word in a name is an indexing unit. Arrange the names in alphabetic order by comparing similar units in each name. Consider the second units only when the first units are identical. Consider the third units only when both the first and second units are identical.

3. **Single Surnames or Initials** A surname, when used alone, precedes the same surname with a first name or initial. A surname with a first initial only precedes a surname with a complete first name. This rule is sometimes stated, "Nothing comes before something."

4. **Surname Prefixes** A surname prefix is *not* a separate indexing unit but it is considered part of the surname. These prefixes include: *d', D', Da, de, De, Del, Des, Di, Du, Fitz, La, Le, M', Mac, Mc, O', St., Van, Van der, Von, Von der*, and others. The prefixes *M', Mac*, and *Mc* are indexed and filed exactly as they are spelled. The prefix *St.* is indexed and filed as though spelled out.

5. **Names of Firms** Names of firms and institutions are indexed and filed exactly as they are written when they do not contain the *complete* name of an individual.

6. **Names of Firms Containing Complete Individual Names** When the firm or institution name includes the *complete* name of an individual, the units are transposed for indexing in the same way as the name of an individual.

7. **Article "The"** When *The* occurs at the beginning of a name, it is placed at the end in parentheses when writing names on cards and folders; if *The* occurs in the middle of a name, it is placed in parentheses but is not moved. In both cases, it is *not* an indexing unit and is disregarded in filing.

8. **Hyphenated Names** Hyphenated firm names are considered as *separate* indexing units. Hyphenated surnames of individuals are considered as *one* indexing unit; this applies also to hyphenated names of individuals whose complete names are part of a firm name.

9. **Abbreviations** Abbreviations are considered as though the name were written in full; however, single letters other than abbreviations are considered as separate indexing units.

in Progressive Filing

RULE

10. **Conjunctions, Prepositions, and Firm Endings** Conjunctions and prepositions, such as *and, for, in, of,* are disregarded in indexing and filing but are not omitted or their order changed when writing names on cards and folders.
    Firm endings, such as *Ltd., Inc., Co., Son, Bros., Mfg.,* and *Corp.,* are treated as a unit in indexing and filing and are considered as though spelled in full, such as *Brothers* and *Incorporated.*

11. **One or Two Words** Names that may be spelled as one word, as two words, or hyphenated are indexed and filed as *one word.*

12. **Compound Geographic Names** Compound geographic names are considered as separate indexing and filing units, except when the first part of the name is not an English word, such as the *Los* in *Los Angeles.*

13. **Titles or Degrees** Titles or degrees of individuals, whether preceding or following the name, are *not* considered in indexing or filing. They are placed in parentheses after the given name or initial. Terms that designate seniority, such as *Jr., Senior, 2nd,* are also placed in parentheses and are considered for indexing and filing only when the names to be indexed are otherwise identical. 6

    Exception A: When the name of an individual consists of a title and one name only, such as *Queen Elizabeth,* it is *not* transposed and the title *is* considered for indexing and filing.

    Exception B: When a title or foreign article is the initial word of a firm or association name, it *is* considered for indexing and filing.

14. **Possessives** When a word ends in *apostrophe s,* the *s* is *not* considered in indexing and filing. However, when a word ends in *s apostrophe,* because the *s* is part of the original word, it *is* considered in indexing and filing. This rule is sometimes stated, "Consider everything up to the apostrophe."

15. **U. S. and Foreign Government Names** Names pertaining to the Federal Government are indexed and filed under *United States Government* and then subdivided by title of the department, bureau, division, commission, or board.
    Names pertaining to foreign governments are indexed and filed under names of countries and then subdivided by title of the department, bureau, division, commission, or board.
    Phrases such as *Department of, Bureau of, Division of, Commission of, Board of,* when used in titles of governmental bodies, are placed in parentheses after the word they modify but are *disregarded* in indexing and filing. Such phrases, however, are considered in indexing and filing nongovernmental names.

Summary of Rules (contd.)

RULE

16. Other Political Subdivisions Names pertaining to other political subdivisions are indexed and filed under the name of the state, county, city, or town, and then subdivided by the title of the department, bureau, division, commission, or board.

17. Numbers Any number in a name is considered as though it were written in words and is indexed and filed as *one* unit.

18. Addresses When the same name appears with different addresses, the names are indexed as usual and arranged alphabetically according to city or town. The state is considered only when there is duplication of both individual or company name and city name. If the same name is located at different addresses within the same city, then the names are arranged alphabetically by streets.

If the same name is located at more than one address on the same street, then the names are arranged from the lower to the higher street number.

19. Bank Names Because the names of many banks are alike in several respects, as *First National Bank, Second National Bank*, etc., banks are indexed and filed first by city location, then by bank name, with the state location written on a card or a folder in parentheses and considered only if necessary.

20. Married Women The legal name of a married woman is the one used for filing purposes. Legally, a man's surname is the only part of a man's name a woman assumes when she marries. Her legal name, therefore, could either be (1) her own first and middle names together with her husband's surname, or (2) her own first name and maiden surname together with her husband's surname. *Mrs.* is placed in parentheses after the name when writing on a card or folder. Her husband's first and middle names are given in parentheses below her legal name.

Index

Abbreviations, 16, 144
Active folders, 45
Addresses, 22, 146
Aids,
 memory, 137-142
 miscellaneous, 89
Alphabetic correspondence filing,
 advantages of, 127
 coding in, 36
 description of, 41
 disadvantages of, 127
 files for, *illus.*, 4, 50, 108, 140
 indexing in, 34-35
 inspection of correspondence in, 34
 materials used in, 42-50
  cabinets, 49-50
  captions, 43-45
  guides, 42, 49
  individual folders, 45-46, 49
  labels, 47-48
  miscellaneous folders, 45-46
 procedure for, 34-39
 sorting in, 36-38
Alphabetic order, 10, 144
Amberg "Nual" Alphabetic Index, 55
Analysis sheet, records, *illus.*, 126
Answer sheet, *illus.*, 13, 26
Arrangement,
 alphabetic, 9-11
 dictionary, 105
 encyclopedic, 105
 of alphabetic file, 49
 of cabinets, *illus.*, 84
 of duplex-numeric subject file, 110
 of geographic file, 99
 of main numeric file, 94; *illus.*, 93
 of subject file, 107-110
Article *the*, 14-15, 144

Bank names, 23, 146
Blueprint file, *illus.*, 83
Borrowed material, follow-up of, 67-68
Businessman, need of files by, 1

Cabinets,
 alphabetic correspondence, 49-50
 microfilm, *illus.*, 77
 selection of, 81-85, 129-131
 special arrangement of, *illus.*, 84
 special records, *illus.*, 83
Captions,
 alphabetic filing, 43-45
 double, or closed, 43; *illus.*, 44
 multiple, 44
 selection of, 34-35
 single, 43-44
 typing of, 47
Card index,
 commercial, 117-122
 cross-reference card, *illus.*, 24
 in geographic filing, 101
 in numeric filing, 95
 nature of, 113-115
 preparation and filing of, 12-24
 typing cards for, 12, 115
 visible, 116-117
Carrier folder, 66
Charge methods, 62-68
Charge-out card, 64-66
Coding,
 description of, 36
 in geographic filing, 102
 in numeric filing, 96
 in subject filing, 111
Color schemes, use of, 52-54, 56, 89

147

148   INDEX

Commercial systems,
  card, 117-122
  description of, 51
  F. E. Bee, 56; *illus.*, 57
  "Safeguard" Index, 56; *illus.*, 57
  Soundex, 117-122
  "Tailor-Made" Index, 58; *illus.*, 59
  Triple-Check Automatic Index, 53-54
  Variadex, 52-53
  Y and E "Direct-Name" Index, 58; *illus.*, 59
Compound geographic names, 17, 145
Conjunctions, 16-17, 144
Correspondence,
  definition of, 30
  routine for handling, 31-33
Control system, 62-68
Cross reference,
  description of, 24, 35
  in card file, *illus.*, 24
  in geographic filing, 101-102
  in numeric filing, 95
  practice in, 25-28
  sheet, *illus.*, 35
    geographic, *illus.*, 101
Cumulative substitution card, 64-66

Date and alphabetic file, *illus.*, 140
Decimal systems, 105-106, 107-110
Degrees, 18-19, 145
Desk-drawer file, *illus.*, 129
Dewey Decimal System, 105-106, 109-110
Dictionary arrangement, 105
"Direct-Name" Index, 58; *illus.*, 59
Double, or closed, captions, 43; *illus.*, 44
Duplex-numeric filing, 106; *illus.*, 110

Encyclopedic arrangement, 105
Equipment and supplies,
  alphabetic correspondence filing, 42-50
  selection of, 80-90, 128-133
    cabinets, 81-85, 129-131
    folders, 86-88, 132-133
    getting advice on, 142

Equipment and supplies (*Continued*)
  selection of (*Continued*)
    guides, 86, 131-132
    miscellaneous aids, 89
    vertical correspondence filing, 30-40
    visible, 85, 116-117
Expansion files, *illus.*, 82

Factory, need of files by, 1
File clerk, skill required by, 6
Filing,
  definition of, 2-3
  importance of, 4-5
  methods of, 6-7
  procedures preliminary to, 31-33
  process, steps in, 34-39
  rules for (*see* Indexing and filing rules)
Firm names and endings, 14, 16-17, 144
FlexiFile, *illus.*, 82, 88
Folders,
  active, 45
  arrangement of,
    in alphabetic filing, 49
    in duplex-numeric subject file, 110
    in geographic filing, 99-100
    in main numeric file, 94; *illus.*, 93
    in subject filing, 107-110
  carrier, 66
  how to file, 38-39
  inactive, 45
  individual, 46
    arrangement of, 49
  labels for, 47-48, 89
  miscellaneous, 45-46, 94
  out, 64-66
  scored, *illus.*, 39
  selection of, 86-88, 132-133
Follow-up, 67-68, 137-142
Foreign government names, 19-20, 145

Geographic correspondence filing,
  advantages of, 127
  arrangement of drawer in, 99
  card index for, 100-101
  coding in, 102
  cross reference in, 101-102
  disadvantages of, 127

Geographic correspondence filing (*Continued*)
  file used in, *illus.*, 6, 100
  folders used in, 99-100
    label for, *illus.*, 47
  indexing in, 102
  inspection of correspondence in, 102
  nature of, 98-99
  procedure for, 102
  sorting in, 102
Geographic names, compound, 17
Government names, 19-20, 145
Guides,
  captions for (*see* Captions)
  in alphabetic filing, 42
    arrangement of, 49
  out, 64-66
  primary, 51
  selection of, 86, 131-132
  special, 51
  staggered, *illus.*, 42, 43

Hyphenated names, 15, 144

Incoming mail, handling of, 31-33
Important papers, retention of, 70
Inactive folders, 45
Index card, *illus.*, 12
Indexing,
  description of, 9-10, 34-35
  in geographic filing, 102
  in numeric filing, 96
  in subject filing, 111
Indexing and filing rules,
  alphabetic arrangement, 9-10
  basic, 10-24
    abbreviations, 16, 144
    addresses, 22, 146
    alphabetic order, 10-11, 144
    article *the*, 15, 144
    bank names, 23, 146
    compound geographic names, 17, 145
    conjunctions, 16-17, 144
    firm names and endings, 14, 16-17, 144
    foreign government names, 19-20, 145

Indexing and filing rules (*Continued*)
  basic (*Continued*)
    hyphenated names, 15, 144
    married women, names of, 23, 146
    names of individuals, 10, 144
    numbers, 21-22, 145
    one or two words, 17, 145
    political subdivisions, 20, 145
    possessives, 19, 145
    prepositions, 16-17, 144
    single surnames or initials, 11, 144
    surname prefixes, 11, 144
    titles or degrees, 18-19, 145
    U. S. Government names, 19-20, 145
  cross reference, 24
  need for standardization of, 8
Individual folders,
  arrangement of, 49
  use of, 46
Individuals, names of, 10, 144
Initials, 11, 144
Inspection of correspondence,
  description of, 34
  in geographic filing, 102
  in numeric filing, 96
  in subject filing, 111
Insurance company, card file used in, *illus.*, 3

Labels,
  preparation of, 47-48
  selection of, 89
Ledger cards, bank, *illus.*, 115

Main numeric file, 92-94
Married women, names of, 23, 146
Materials (*see* Equipment and supplies)
Memory helpers, 137-142
Microcard, 79
Microfilming, 76-79
Miscellaneous folders, 45-46, 94
Multiple caption, 44
Multisort, *illus.*, 38

Names,
  bank, 23, 146
  compound geographic, 17, 145
  firm, 14, 144

150 INDEX

Names (*Continued*)
  government, 19-20, 145
  hyphenated, 15, 144
  of individuals, 10, 144
  of married women, 23, 146
Nonessential records, 70
Notations (*see* Captions)
Numbers, 22, 145
Numeric correspondence filing,
  advantages of, 128
  coding in, 96
  disadvantages of, 128
  duplex, 106; *illus.*, 110
  file used in, *illus.*, 5
  folder label for, *illus.*, 47
  indexing in, 96
  inspection of correspondence in, 96
  nature of, 91-92
  organization of, 92-95
  procedure for, 95-96
  significant number systems of, 96
  sorting in, 96
  terminal digit systems of, 96

Office worker, importance of filing to, 5
One or two words, 17, 145
Open-shelf file, 129; *illus.*, 130
Out guides and folders, 64-66; *illus.*, 65

Periodic transfer, 72-75; *illus.*, 73, 74
Permanent records, 70-71
Perpetual transfer, 75
Photographing machine, microfilm, *illus.*, 78
Political subdivisions, 20, 145
Possessives, 19, 145
Prefixes, surname, 11, 144
Preliminary procedures, 31-33
Prepositions, 16-17, 144
Primary guide, 51
Procedures,
  attention to, 133-136
  coding, 36, 96, 102, 111
  geographic filing, 102
  indexing, 34-35, 96, 102, 111
  inspecting, 34, 96, 102, 111
  numeric filing, 95-96

Procedures (*Continued*)
  preliminary, 31-33
  sorting, 36-38, 96, 102, 111
  subject filing, 111
  vertical correspondence filing, 30-40
Professional men, need of files by, 2

Records,
  analysis sheet, *illus.*, 126
  nonessential, 70
  permanent, 70-71
  retention of (*see* Retention of records)
  types of, 3-4
Relative index, 106-107
Requests for filed material, handling, 63
Requisition slip, 64-66
Retention of records,
  for one year, 72
  for seven years, 71
  from two to three years, 71-72
  important papers, 70
  nonessential papers, 70
  permanent, 70-71
  provision for, 136-137
  useful papers, 70
  vital papers, 70
Rotary equipment, *illus.*, 85
Rules (*see* Indexing and filing rules)

Safeguard" Index, 56; *illus.*, 57
Scored folders, *illus.*, 39
Secretary, importance of filing to, 4-5
Significant number systems, 96
Single guide captions, 43
Single surname, 11, 144
Sorting,
  description of, 36-38
  in geographic filing, 102
  in numeric filing, 96
  in subject filing, 111
  tray, *illus.*, 38
Soundex, 117-122
Special guide, 51
Special records cabinet, *illus.*, 83
Staggered guides, *illus.*, 42, 43
Subdivisions, political, 20

Subject correspondence filing,
  advantages of, 127
  alphabetic, 105; *illus.*, 108
    file arrangement in, 107
  coding in, 111
  decimal systems of, 105-106, 107-110
  dictionary arrangement in, 105
  disadvantages of, 127
  duplex-numeric, 106; *illus.*, 110
  encyclopedic arrangement in, 105
  folder label for, *illus.*, 47
  file for, *illus.*, 7
  indexing in, 111
  inspection of correspondence in, 111
  nature of, 104-105
  numeric, 105-106; *illus.*, 108
    file arrangement in, 107-110
  procedure for, 111
  relative index in, 106-107
  sorting in, 111
  subject classification in, 106-107
Substitution cards, 64-66
Super-Filer, *illus.*, 82
Surname, 11, 144
Systems,
  Commercial (*see* Commercial systems)
  decimal, 105-106, 107-110
  establishment and maintenance of, 124-143

Tailor-Made" Index, 58; *illus.*, 59
Terminal digit systems, 96
The, how to file, 15

Tickler file, 67; *illus.*, 64
Time-stamping, 31; *illus.*, 32
Titles, 18-19, 145
Transfer methods,
  boxes used in, *illus.*, 71
  microfilming useful in, 76-79
  need for, 69-70
  periodic, 72-75; *illus.*, 73, 74
  perpetual, 75
Triple-Check Automatic Index, 53-54; *colored illus.*
Two-tier letter tray, *illus.*, 33
Typing,
  captions, 47
  cards, 12, 115

Unit, definition of, 9
U. S. Government names, 19-20, 145
U. S. War Department Decimal Classification, 109
Useful papers, retention of, 70

Variadex System, 52-53; *colored illus.*
V-cut pocket file, *illus.*, 82
Vertical correspondence filing, 30-40
Visible equipment, 85, 116-117
Vital papers, retention of, 70

Williams Decimal Classification, 109
Words, one or two, 17, 145

Y and E "Direct-Name" Index, 58; *illus.*, 59